D0839734

ALONE ON THE BATTLEFIELD

Kirk House Publishers

ALONE ON THE BATTLEFIELD

A CHILD SURVIVING
THE KOREAN WAR

HYON KIM

Alone on the Battlefield: A Child Surviving the Korean War © Copyright 2022 Hyon Kim

All rights reserved. No part of this book may be used or reproduced in any manner whatsoever without written permission of the author except in the case of brief quotations embodied in critical articles and reviews.

The information in this book is distributed as an "as is" basis, without warranty. Although every precaution has been taken in the preparation of this work, neither the author nor the publisher shall have any liability to any person or entity with respect to any loss or damage caused or alleged to be caused directly or indirectly by the information contained in this book.

First Edition

978-1-952976-46-9 paperback
978-1-952976-47-6 eBook
978-1-952976-48-3 hardcover

Library of Congress Control Number: 2022906387

Cover and interior designed by: Ann Aubitz

Published by Kirk House Publishers
1250 E 115th Street
Burnsville, MN 55337
Kirkhousepublishers.com
612-781-2815

TABLE OF CONTENTS

ACKNOWLEDGMENT

I have many to thank for helping me realize this vision.

I thank my dear Lord God and Jesus for His protection.

I have endless love for my two sons who have supported me and given me courage: Paul, who is a proud father of three, and Chris, who spent countless hours helping me translate and edit this book.

I am deeply grateful to my writer and producer friend, Mr. Lee Sang-hoon, and many of my other dear friends for their constant encouragement to help this book come out into the world.

I would also like to thank Ms. Jung Hyun-mi of Oneness Media for helping me release this book in Korea.

Finally, I would like to dedicate this book to my father and mother, who have gone to heaven. I also dedicate it to the memory of my younger brother, who was only two years old when we were first parted and has now passed from this earth.

PROLOGUE: ON MY WAY HOME

It was a long journey indeed. One day in June of 1950, I grabbed my grandmother's hand, hopped down the stone stairs of my house in Seoul, and traveled to my aunt's home in a southern province.

A few days later, on June 25, 1950, the Korean War began, and the world was turned into a sea of blood. My mother and two brothers had no choice but to leave Seoul and follow my father to North Korea. At four years old, I was left behind, alone on the battlefield.

Not only was I left behind, but I was also given a label, a shameful epithet that would follow me: *bbal-gang-i*. It meant I was a "red," a "commie," *a piece of shit*. It also meant that I was marked for death. My father was a communist—so people also thought of me as one.

More than seventy years have passed since that day. From that time on, my hatred, my utter despisal of my father is a pain that I have carried. This hatred I had for him was even more vile than the label of bbal-gang-i that I had to endure. My father never came back for me. I have hated my father my entire life from the moment he went to North Korea with my family—and left me behind.

Father, you have been dead since 1956. Your body is tangled anonymously among many corpses underneath the concrete of a street with no name in North Korea. I was heartbroken whenever I thought of you. I hated you and I missed you.

Yet even in the dim memories of my childhood, the warmth you showed me when we were together shines through. I remembered how you would call me your princess. I remember your loving eyes as you hugged me many times a day. Often, I still feel like that four-year-old girl trying to hold her father tight. It is only now, in my old age, that I have begun to remove the stigma of being a bbal-gang-i—a red, a communist. It is only now that I am trying to erase the feeling of hatred that I have built up in my heart. Now I want to tell the story of what I needed to do to survive and how I longed to live in my father's arms.

Now I think I can find my own way home.

CHAPTER ONE

My earliest childhood memory was of being woken up by the sounds of war, the horrible *boom, boom, boom* of cannon fire. It was a hot summer night in 1950. I was four years old. While I tried to sleep, the distant booms echoed in my ears, getting louder and louder, coming closer, like a dark mountain shadow. I was very scared, and I wanted to get out of bed and scream for my father, but I was so far away from him. I was with my maternal grandmother at my aunt's house, many miles away. My mother's sister scolded me and said that I could not cry out for my father. I swallowed my screams and just listened to the ominous booms.

My aunt said, "Mother, I think the sound of the artillery fire is getting closer! I will put the child on my back. You put the bundles on your head and follow me quickly."

In a flash, my aunt scrambled around the house, put me on her back, and gathered together a bundle of belongings, which my grandmother put on her head. My poor grandmother was sobbing softly.

"Mother, please do not worry," my aunt said. "I have already arranged for us to escape to the mountain village. We are going to Jungsoo's home. I gave her some money and a large sack of rice. They will be waiting for us."

We all ran out the back door of my aunt's house and disappeared into the darkness. That was how the three of us hurriedly escaped into the wilderness in the dead of night.

My aunt was upset. "My husband has already run off to hide with his concubine, and I don't even know where he is!"

"He's an awful man! Tossing his wife aside and running off while all of this is happening!" my grandmother whispered angrily.

As my aunt quickly walked down the dark path in the night, she said, breathlessly, "After my husband found out that the child's father is a bbal-gang-i, he treats us both like lepers. And it's not just him; the whole village treats us like that. They are especially cruel to the child. Until the war is over and the world has changed, we will have to hide deep in the mountains."

As we walked, the small road disappeared into a mountain trail.

During the entire summer of 1950, we lived in a tiny mountain village deep in the valley with Jung-soo's family, who were longtime friends with my mother. Even during these dangerous times, there were good people, and we were grateful for their kindness.

I remember eating watermelon with Jung-soo under the shade of a small wooden overhang. We would play *ddakji,* a game with folded paper similar to Pogs in America, with the village children. We would break up hard clumps of dirt to find edible kudzu roots. In the middle of this bloody war, I would sit and watch the clouds floating peacefully over the mountains.

Sometimes, my aunt would leave me with my grandmother and go back to her home in town. When she did this, I would wait endlessly at the entrance to the small village for her return. As soon as I saw her, I would run to my grandmother to tell her my aunt was coming. My grandmother would then take out the cooked rice she had stashed under a blanket in the warmest corner in the room and set the table for my aunt and us to eat.

Whenever the three of us would sit at that tiny table, my thoughts would be with my family in Seoul—my parents, my brothers, all of us together as a family. I missed those evenings when the entire family would gather, happily bustling about.

Whenever my aunt would return from town, she cautiously spoke to my grandmother, hoping others would not hear. She would whisper dark news of the war in her ear.

In Seoul, the South Korean army had blown up the bridge over the Han River in order to delay the North Korean military from coming further south. This action trapped many people in Seoul, who were then captured by the North Koreans.

In September, General MacArthur landed at Incheon and recaptured Seoul for the South. It was then that my grandmother traveled to Seoul to look for our family.

"I am alone, grandma is gone, and daddy doesn't know where I am now! What if he can't find me?" I was so worried while I waited for my aunt to return from town. When I saw her from a distance, I jumped for joy. As soon as she returned, my aunt hurriedly cooked the rice just as my grandmother had. I wonder if I understood then that this sense of hunger would settle in my heart for the rest of my life.

My aunt said I was always an excellent eater. Because I was very young, I would sit at our tiny dining table, stuff my mouth full of rice, and hastily eat it all. My aunt would watch me with pity in her heart, holding back tears, and say, "You poor thing! Your bbal-gang-i father did this to you! The devil himself has done this!" She would sigh and look at me with tears welling up in her eyes.

During the thirty-five-year Japanese occupation, after the fall of the Joseon dynasty in 1910, the Korean people were degraded, tortured, and humiliated by the Japanese occupiers. The Koreans were finally able to escape the clutches of Japanese rule, but before the deep wounds of the nation had even healed, Korea's greatest tragedy, the Korean War, began on June 25, 1950, our date of infamy. Despite the two sides signing an armistice in 1953, the Korean War has never formally come to an end. Thus, the two sides remain at war. No one ever thought that this tragic war would still continue over seventy years later.

During this awful war, there were more civilian deaths than soldier deaths. Additionally, with so many foreign troops involved on both sides, Korean women were regularly raped and assaulted in both rural and urban areas.

I have talked to friends that still vividly remember these tragic times.

My friend Yong-mi, who lived in Seoul with her family, was trapped in the city when the war broke out in June, and she could not evacuate until the United Nations forces freed Seoul on September 28, 1950. The people in Seoul had to endure so much hardship at that time, and she lost many family members.

Her uncle was a captain in the youth military in Yeongsan Township before the war. He was not able to evacuate, so he went into hiding. However, the North Korean forces eventually forced him out of hiding and executed him on the spot, shooting him in the face. According to Yong-mi, during the retreat of United Nations forces on January 4, 1951, "the South Korean police were going from house to house, evacuating people and putting a red sticker on the front gates to indicate the house was clear. They urged us to evacuate soon. They said that Chinese soldiers would come into our homes and rape the women. They said we would be stabbed and killed no matter who we were. Even a child or an elderly woman would be stabbed and killed. They frightened us so that we would leave Seoul as quickly as possible."

But as she describes it, escaping the Chinese soldiers did not mean escaping tragedy. Her other uncle's wife and mother of three children were raped by an American soldier shortly after her husband had left to fight with the Korean National Guard. She became pregnant, but she thought the baby belonged to her husband because she had spent a few nights with him before he left. When she gave birth, it became clear that it was the baby of the soldier who had raped her. At that time in Korea, having a mixed-race child brought immense shame to the family.

When her husband returned, he believed that there was nothing to be done except raise the child with his wife as his own. While he was a decent, good-hearted man, many of his relatives were more closed-minded. Yong-mi's aunt became an outcast among her in-laws. She took great care in raising her child but was treated like a woman of sin. Her in-laws spat on the ground with contempt when they saw her. They looked down on her and did not allow her to participate in ancestral worship ceremonies.

It was difficult for the child as well, with enormous discrimination against mixed-race kids in Korean society. They were not even allowed to join the military. Military service was required in Korea, and without having served in the military, it was nearly impossible to get a job.

In the 1980s, as president of the Korean American Women's Association in the United States, I visited an orphanage in the city of Bupyeong, South Korea, with a photographer and a former American football player. The orphanage was run by an American Maryknoll priest named Father Benedict Zweber, who took us around the country, from the demilitarized zone (DMZ) at the North Korean border to Busan, down on the southern coast.

As we traveled, we interviewed several mixed-race, fatherless children, known as "Amerasians," and made a series of videos. These were all children of American soldiers. Other than a couple of success stories of people who had become successful pop music singers, they all had miserable lives dominated by extreme discrimination and hardship. It was worse for the females, many of whom resorted to selling their bodies. As we visited all these Amerasians, I became very angry at how they were being treated by Korean society.

We produced ten videos, then took the footage and edited it into one presentation that we sent to President Ronald Reagan. We explained that these Amerasian orphans were the children left behind by American soldiers who had fought bravely in the Korean War. We explained that these children were Americans.

Our work, alongside that of many other human rights activists, resulted in President Reagan signing legislation in 1982 to make it easier for Asian-born children of American soldiers to come to the United States.

We wanted these Amerasians—these *Americans*—to have the opportunity to be free of the icy gaze of Korean society and live proudly in the United States.

During the Korean War, countless women were raped by foreign soldiers, Chinese soldiers, and even Korean soldiers. During the night, in many houses the women hid under the floorboards while the men stood guard outside. As Yong-mi's family was evacuating, they stayed at a farmhouse where everyone, farmers and laborers alike, lived together. The wife of one of the farmhands was considered homely, so she used to say to people, "There is no way an ugly woman like me could ever get raped." She did not hide under the floorboards and went around freely without fear. One day, an American soldier came and raped her right in front of her husband. Yong-mi, who was eight years old at the time, witnessed the whole thing, and she was so scared that she could not even scream. The soldier made the woman undress in front of her husband at gunpoint and then raped her. It was such an awful and sad scene. She cried in fear, and her husband could do nothing to help her—so they both just wept.

Yong-mi's family moved on to Suwon in the freezing weather and started heading south, toward Daejeon. The traveling conditions were so cruel and terrifying that her mother said she could not go any further, and they returned to Seoul. Her mother said that if they were going to die, she would rather do it at home. They joined others who also seemed to be returning to Seoul. When they got to the Han River, they crossed it by boat.

They would often walk along the train tracks. The train carrying refugees south would come upon them without notice. Alongside the tracks was a long procession of people carrying heavy bundles on their heads and backs, pulling small wagons, and sometimes carrying the sick and elderly. They were all traveling south.

One day, when the train stopped at the station, people swarmed like bees around the train cars, pushing and shoving to get on, some climbing onto the roof, everyone packing themselves together. As the train got ready to proceed, bombs suddenly fell from the sky. Yong-mi was only eight years old when she saw the countless mutilated and dead bodies strewn about the tracks. This gave her nightmares, and she was unable to sleep at night.

As she was telling me these stories, she paused to let out a long sad sigh as she contemplated the pain of this continued reality, saying "there are still two countries where there was once one—North and South Korea."

She remembered the sad songs they sang as children and began singing about that experience in the most heart-wrenching words— emotions she remembered so clearly.

> *Father was evacuated and then died.*
> *Our house has burned down.*
> *There is no place for our family to go.*
> *My older brother is off to join the army of the North.*
> *My younger brother is off to join the army of the South.*
> *Shoot your guns and kill.*
> *The Jiri Mountain red army . . .*

She trailed off. "I have forgotten the rest."

Then she started another song:

> *Today the planes went overhead, two by two,*
> *Carrying bombs to the North*
> *To drop on the red cattle dreaming of aggression.*
> *Not missing anyone.*
> *Fighting bravely.*
> *Carrying the bombs.*
> *We will win.*
> *We must win.*
> *Win and come back.*
> *Carrying the bombs.*

During this time, many communist guerrillas lived in the Jiri Mountain region of the South Chungcheong and Jeolla provinces. Police caught and jailed another one of Yong-mi's uncles on suspicion of making ammunition for the communist guerrilla army. The jailed uncle's wife took nearly forty communist guerrilla soldiers into the Sacheon police station to try and rescue her husband—and they all were shot and killed in a bloodbath.

Because of this, Yong-mi's cousin lost his parents and had to survive alone; however, because his parents had assisted the communists, the government seized his family's land. It made life in South Korea very difficult for him, and he could not attend school or get steady work for the rest of his life.

I would have had similar struggles because of my father becoming a communist if my aunt had not officially registered me as her daughter.

One day in June of 1950, I went with my grandmother to visit my aunt's house in the country. I say "my aunt's house," but it seems more appropriate to call it my uncle's house or even my aunt's husband's house. My aunt, who had not given birth to a son, had to struggle to maintain her status as the head woman of the house.

I was excited to visit my aunt. Her house was in a village on the outskirts of Puyo. When I arrived there at the end of a long journey with my grandmother, my aunt frowned when she saw me. "Mother, why did you bring this girl and not her older brother?"

My grandmother wrapped her skirt around me and said, "We are going to go home soon. We ran out of food, and I am here to get some rice. This little one is so hungry for rice. Your sister asked me to bring her here and feed her."

My aunt's face softened a little, and she hurried to prepare us food to eat. "Welcome, Mother, I have not seen you in a long time. I was going to travel up to Seoul soon. You must be very tired. It is a long way to travel. Let's eat. Are you hungry?"

My grandmother put a spoon in my hand so I could eat first. Every time I put some rice on the spoon, she would add a little bit of food from one of the side dishes onto it.

My aunt looked at me and said, "You sit very politely and eat nicely. I can see your mother taught you well."

My grandmother sighed with tears in her eyes. "Her mother has always been a first-rate teacher. Sadly, she has been fired from her school."

"How are you all doing?"

"We rarely see her father's face anymore. He is always hiding from the police. And her mother is helping out with the Catholic nuns. They don't care whether our family is communist or not. We all got baptized as Catholics after the Methodists kicked us out of their church. Her Catholic name is Maria. I am Anna. Your sister is Teresa. Her father is Peter. And the boys are Paul and John."

Here is why I consider my aunt to be my second mother:

While my mother was pregnant with me, she had a dream about picking up a baby turtle as she walked along the beach. As she was carrying it home, she became worried that my brother might hurt the turtle while playing with it. Suddenly, her sister appeared before her. My mother was very worried about bringing the baby turtle home, so she put it into her sister's skirt and asked her to take care of it instead.

After I was born, my mother always worried in her heart that if I stayed with her, I would not live a long life. She wanted me to call my aunt "Mom" and be close to her.

When the police found out that my father was a communist, my parents lost their jobs. It became very difficult for us to survive. My father was a good family man and a great father to us, but he was wanted by the police and often had to go into hiding.

Sometimes my mother would help him, speaking to people and promoting communist ideals. One time the police arrested her with my father and locked them up with my baby brother.

But I was a child and knew nothing about these hardships. I had held my mother's hand every day and demanded that she feed us rice three times a day. I would cry out for my father and always look for him. I was an annoying little troublemaker.

One day, while my father was away, hiding from the police, my mother could not take it anymore, and she had complained to my grandmother. "Mother, please take my daughter to my sister's house and bring back some rice and things to eat. Feed her as much rice as she can eat. If her father finds out I am sending her away, he will scold me. Hurry, please hurry, Mother."

That one decision changed my destiny.

So, at my aunt's house, in June 1950, my grandmother became so emotional talking to my aunt that she could not eat properly. After dinner, they continued to talk into the night.

At one point, I heard my aunt raise her voice. "But Mother, you know my situation. Not only have I not birthed a son, but the one daughter I did have died within a year. Now my life here is a living hell. My husband openly walks around the village with a concubine—and is trying to bring her into the house to live with us. Two women living in the same house with one man." My aunt turned to look at me. "If she was a boy, I could justify it. Adopting a son might help my situation, but adopting that useless girl is just a burden."

Perhaps my aunt forgot that even though I was a child, I had eyes with which to see and ears with which to listen. Just like that, at the age of four, I went from being the bossy girl in the neighborhood who took care of her brothers and was worshipped by her father to being a good-for-nothing piece of trash that was of no use to anyone.

Adults forget that children, no matter how young, have eyes that can see, ears that can hear, and hearts that can break. Adults carelessly spit out words that stab at the small hearts of children. Those wounds do not always heal. Those wounds can remain forever. When I was living in my aunt's house, I suffered immeasurable pain and was scarred for life.

My grandmother spoke angrily about my aunt's husband, not knowing that I was listening. "What a terrible man he is. My daughter, come to Seoul with me. Let us get some fresh air and relax, away from him."

As they exchanged these words, they had no way of knowing that in a few days, the tragedy of June 25, 1950, the beginning of the Korean War, was coming. And that it would be one of the most devastating disasters to ever befall the Korean people. War is always the greatest tragedy for humans—and yet war is always created by humans.

***

Five years earlier, on the morning of August 15, 1945, World War II was coming to an end, and Emperor Hirohito announced the surrender of Japan. Even then, Joseph Stalin was already scheming about creating a communist Korean peninsula as he did to Eastern Europe.

Declassified documents released nearly fifty years later in 1993 show that on September 20, 1945, shortly after the end of World War II, Stalin issued an order to make North Korea a communist regime. As outlined in an article in the *Dong-A* newspaper on February 26, 1993, these documents made it clear that the Soviet Union envisioned a communist government for the whole of Korea shortly after the North Korean occupation.

Stalin appointed Kim Il-sung as a captain in the Soviet army and an immediate subordinate to himself, so they could work together to promote the North Korean communist agenda.

During World War II, British Prime Minister Winston Churchill and American President Franklin Delano Roosevelt worked with the villainous Stalin to defeat the even more monstrous Adolf Hitler. However, Stalin used his victories in Eastern Europe to solidify and increase a communist bloc of nations—often through cruel tactics.

For four years the United States fought a difficult, bloody war along the Japanese front of World War II. And not until days before the very end of the conflict did Stalin respond to pleas for assistance with Soviet troops. Thus, when the United States finally defeated Japan, Stalin was there just in time to share the credit.

World War II began on September 1, 1939, in Europe, and ended on September 2, 1945, with Japan's official surrender. The Soviet Union was among the "big three" allied powers that were the key to victory in the war, along with England and the United States. China also played a major part. The leaders of these powers met throughout the war in Cairo, Tehran, and Yalta to discuss strategy and determine how the conquered territories would be organized after the war. Stalin was distrustful and angry because he did not think he would get the territories he wanted—so he strategized ways to get Manchuria and the Korean peninsula in his clutches.

Toward the end of the war, under Stalin's command, Soviet troops bulldozed their way through Manchuria and into Korea to drive out Japanese forces. The United States' forces, which were in Okinawa at the time, were concerned by how quickly Stalin was moving. In their view, Soviet troops were ready to descend all the way to Busan on the southeastern tip of the Korean peninsula.

The United States quickly proposed dividing Korea into two occupation zones, with the thirty-eighth parallel as a border. Fortunately, Stalin accepted this arrangement and withdrew his army north. The quick thinking in establishing the thirty-eighth parallel as a border was critical in saving the South from Stalin and a Soviet occupation.

Stalin immediately reinforced the border and deployed Soviet troops along the thirty-eighth parallel. He cut off all means of transportation, including railways. He halted any operations between the North and South. Residents were not even allowed to cross the border to walk back to their hometowns.

In 1948, Soviet troops even prevented United Nations election watchers in Seoul from traveling north of the thirty-eighth parallel. The United Nations Temporary Commission, whose task was to supervise free and open elections, was not allowed to visit North Korea, and Stalin also worked to interfere with the general elections in the South.

This border that Stalin created has cut the Korean peninsula in half (at its waist) for over seventy years.

Just as Stalin had fought off Nazi Germany and then occupied and forced communism into the countries of Poland, Czechoslovakia, Romania, Bulgaria, Croatia, Bosnia, and Serbia, he tried hard to quickly make Korea a communist country. Stalin worked with North Korean leader Kim Il-sung and China's Mao Zedong to reunify the entire Korean peninsula under one communist government. It is regrettable that

Korea's neighbors, Stalin and Mao Zedong, were two of history's most ruthless dictators and committers of genocide.

Stalin was notorious for mercilessly squashing any of his critics to remain in power during his rule. History has judged his reign as the most brutal dictatorship of the twentieth century. According to Naomi Wolf, an American writer and journalist, Stalin studied Hitler very closely.

From 1936 to 1938, during what is now known as the Great Purge, Stalin committed extremely violent acts of political repression. His actions constituted a massacre under the guise of maintaining law and order. More than 700,000 people were shot to death, and more than 2 million people were sent to forced labor camps after being tortured by the secret police. It is estimated that between 950,000 and 1.2 million people were executed or died in prison over a two-year period. The number of people who were tortured and sent to labor prison camps in Siberia exceeds even that.

These deaths included Korean independence activists like General Kim Kyung-cheon, a major force in the armed anti-Japanese struggle, and Park Jin-soon, a Stalin puppet in the early days but also a pioneer of the Korean socialist independence movement.

Some estimate that through purging, combat, and famine, Stalin was responsible for around twenty-two million deaths until his death in 1953. This number excludes all those who perished in the Korean War.

Now, what about Mao Zedong? How many people were oppressed and killed under him? The reckless authoritarian policies of Mao are exemplified by his Cultural Revolution, a sociopolitical purge estimated to have caused between twenty and thirty million deaths in China. In addition to the great human cost, these policies also brought harm to China's cultural, social, economic, and diplomatic well-being.

Mao Zedong was a ruthless and violent dictator who slaughtered people and destroyed China's social structure. Mao's Great Leap Forward of the late 1950s and early 1960s completely restructured China's economy into what were called "the people's communes." This policy was an economic disaster, and it caused one of the largest famines in history that resulted in anywhere from twenty to fifty million deaths. It is estimated that around seventy-five million people died under the rule of Mao Zedong.

Juche (sometimes translated as "self-reliance") is considered the official ideology of North Korea. It is a rhetorical ideology developed by Kim Il-sung to justify his absolute dictatorship—and has been in practice for over seventy years. It unfairly justifies the government's repressive policies as necessary for Korea's self-reliance.

Juche elevates communist ideals—like the denial of private property and eliminating the gap between rich and poor. In reality, there is still a large gap between the powerful and the powerless, and many people have died of poverty and starvation under this communist one-party dictatorship.

Today, much of twentieth-century communism and its Marxist/Leninist ideals have crumbled. The Soviet Union and the communist regimes of Eastern Europe have fallen, meaning the fate of the remaining communist regimes are in a precarious position.

On June 25, 1950, the Korean War broke out. As planned by Stalin and Kim Il-sung, Mao Zedong supported the war effort with the Chinese army. The fighting lasted three years, one month, and two days, causing countless tragedies. It is awful to have a war in which you are fighting and killing your own people. Brother fought against brother, and yet it was all because of forces outside of Korea's control—this is the great tragedy of this war. Stalin died on March 5, 1953. An armistice agreement was drafted and signed at Panmunjom that July. It put an end to the fighting but technically did not end the war. Korea is the only remaining divided nation in the world. It has been in a civil war for over seventy years.

On the morning of August 15, 1945, when the Japanese announced their surrender, Koreans poured into the streets to celebrate, waving the *Tae-guk-gi* flag of Korea. They shouted in celebration of their independence until their voices became hoarse.

My aunt, who lived in the countryside, was also excited and ran through the streets, waving the *Tae-guk-gi* flag and cheering.

My mother, a teacher, no longer needed to visit the Japanese shrine. I often think about how happy she must have been to finally be able to teach her students in Korean and call them by their Korean names.

But as people were waving the Korean flag in every corner of the country, I am certain my father's heart was filled with his dream of building a new communist government in Korea.

Because of the beliefs of my father, the tragic path of my life became irreversible for me, my siblings, and my highly educated mother. It is heartbreaking that the tragedy of our family was created by my father's actions and his communist ideology.

***

My father was born in 1920, during the oppressive Japanese colonial period of Korean history. He graduated from Bae Jae Christian High School and studied at the prestigious Gyeongsang National University.

His mother, my grandmother, who was a deaconess with the Methodist church, was a strong woman. She worked in an American missionary's house to make money and raise my father. She had a difficult life because of her irresponsible, parasitic husband, who drank and chased women all the time and never worked.

The student life for my father was not easy. During the Japanese occupation, only a few Korean students were at Gyeongsang University. Most of the professors and students were Japanese.

One day, my father got into a fight with a Japanese student who was always disparaging and harassing my father. He often called my father derogatory names that the Japanese had for Koreans. There are dire consequences for a Korean who fights with a Japanese student, and my father had hurt him severely.

The Japanese police nearly beat my father to death at the police station, but they did eventually free him. After this incident, my father fled to China.

I know very little of father's life during this time. I do not know what sorts of difficulties he encountered in China. I do not know when or how he became involved with other exiled Koreans in the Korean Independence Movement. I do not know when and how he began to favor a communist ideology. What is clear to me, however, is that my father's communist ideals eventually brought catastrophe upon my mother and our family.

When my father returned from China, his mother introduced him to a woman, my mother, who was a lay minister at their Methodist church.

My mother was a modern, educated woman who graduated from the Christian Women's College in Pyongyang. She chose a Christian college because she did not want to bow at a Japanese shrine. She refused to study abroad in Tokyo.

My mother and father fell in love, married, and began raising a family. My father worked at the now world-famous Samsung Trading Company, and my mother was a primary school teacher. We were a relatively affluent household in Seoul.

When I was born in 1946, my country had just come out of the thirty-five years of brutality that was the Japanese colonial period. My country was like a child who had not yet learned to walk.

At my home, I was the only daughter. While sons are very essential to Korean society, I was viewed as the precious daughter, positioned between my two brothers in age. I received an abundance of love and affection from my father. He thought I was precious and always called me his beautiful princess. He loved to put me on his shoulders and play with me at home. He would proudly carry me around. I had a happy childhood with my father, playing all the time and acting the part of a little captain or princess in my home.

My father was a warm-hearted man with a great personality. In our house, my father took care of my maternal grandmother, who had no sons, only four daughters. Every few months, my father would send freshly caught fish to my aunt in Puyo. He also supported my other aunts and cousins in Seoul.

The joy of our liberation from the brutality of Japanese rule passed quickly as our country's fate was once again being determined by others. We stood in the dangerous position of being a pawn between the superpowers of the United States, the Soviet Union, and China.

The United States tried and failed to work with the moderate Koreans. Dr. Syngman Rhee was trying to establish a democratic government of the Republic of Korea through the United Nations. Mr. Kim Gu opposed the Soviet-US trusteeship and the dividing of Korea. This put him at odds with the US military. The Workers' Party of South Korea was also openly fighting with the US military. All these entities found themselves in conflict. While the leaders on the Korean peninsula were fighting against each other, Stalin was planning to stoke the fires of these conflicts and Korean ideas of nationalism to create a communist Korea, just as he had done in Eastern Europe.

The tragedy of history cast a black shadow over our families too. Just after I turned one hundred days old, my father came home, held me in his arms, and cried, "Our princess!" My father was a good family man happily raising his children—but at the same time, he was a supporter of Stalin. He was a member of the Workers' Party of South Korea, which worked toward Stalin's goal of a communist Korea, often resorting to violence and terrorism.

Where was my beloved father when all of this was happening?

What acts did he commit during this time?

Was my father involved in acts against the US military?

In my aunt's recollection, my father was always being chased by the police. When he went into hiding, he would take all his worn-out books with him, especially the books by Karl Marx. He would pack the books before grabbing anything he might actually need, like clothes.

Sometimes, he would sneak past the police and meet my aunt at a small market restaurant. His face would be beaming as he quickly ate a simple bowl of soup. He wanted very little, and this simple meal would make him smile.

I still cannot believe that my father, a Christian, was a follower of the devilish Stalin. I have lived my life with deep sorrow and resentment toward my father for the foolish things he did—and for his misguided belief in someone who helped lead my country into the fearsome path of war.

For most of my life, I could not forgive my father for loving the Communist Party more than his family. During those troubled times in my country, he would have been much more valuable as a good husband and father than as an idealist and a communist.

After Seoul was recaptured by the South Korean forces on September 28, 1950, we returned from the mountain village to my aunt's town of Puyo. When we arrived, a man who had known my parents in Seoul shouted in front of all the townspeople, "I was not able to evacuate because the Korean military destroyed the Han River Bridge, and I almost died while in hiding. But her father"—he pointed at me— "was a devoted communist, and before Seoul was restored to the South, he took his family to the North. Their family is all bbal-gang-i!"

After hearing this man's accusatory words about my father, my aunt's face flushed red with anger. "No! This is not true!" she cried. "Are you really going to believe that opium addict? Who knows what things he may have done in Seoul?"

When my grandmother had witnessed this exchange, she started packing the moment we arrived at my aunt's house. She wanted to see for herself whether my father and his family had truly fled North.

"Daughter, I cannot stay here. I must go to Seoul!"

"Mother, where are you going, in the middle of this war?"

"Your sister would not have gone north without us! I am going to Seoul to see it with my own eyes. I will leave my granddaughter here with you."

So, my grandmother left me behind and went to Seoul. Her journey was a dangerous one filled with war and death. As everyone else was struggling to head south, my grandmother, in the middle of a war, went north to check on my family in Seoul and see if they had fled to North Korea—or if they were even alive.

The war had destroyed the entire nation. People's lives were devastated. They were living worse than worms. After my grandmother went to Seoul, she told my aunt that she had seen dead bodies all along the roads. Everyone was constantly terrified, and at any moment bombs could fall out of the sky and explode. My grandmother said she cried and trembled from witnessing so much death.

Once she saw a family casually eating a meal next to a decaying corpse. Another time, she saw a baby crawling among the dead bodies, crying for his dead mother's milk. Just like in Yong-mi's story, she too witnessed the chaos and struggle of everyone at the train stations and saw the devastation from the bombs as they tore the train and the people to pieces.

But the thing that made my grandmother most afraid was the fact that she could not trust anyone she encountered. The war turned ordinary people into monsters who would kill each other just to survive.

By the time my grandmother arrived in Seoul, she had encountered death countless times, and when she finally arrived at my parents' house, its gate hanging open, she sat down in exhaustion and despair. My father had indeed taken my family north before the UN forces had come and restored Seoul, and he abandoned me and my grandmother in the countryside of Puyo. Knowing that he chose to do this devastated me for decades—and I have never stopped resenting him for this.

Not only did I have to endure this terrible war without my family, but also with this name—*his* name, the name of a bbal-gang-i, a dirty red commie—was the one thing he left behind for me.

Over forty years later, I heard the story of what had happened. My father came home, out of hiding, to pick up his family and bring them north—but I was missing. When he found out, he was enraged and full of despair, beating on his chest. My mother said he never forgave her for sending me away to the Puyo countryside with my grandmother.

Before they left for the north, my father made a large package of photos of my family and gave it to my other aunt in Seoul so I would have them. At my father's request, she gave the package of photos to my aunt.

But my aunt banned me from telling anyone about my family once she had learned that they had fled north. Growing up, I did not even know the names of my father and mother. Regardless, I will always cherish the memories of when, on days that were especially lonely and awful, I would retrieve that package of photos from deep in my aunt's cabinet and relive my family's happy memories. It was a taboo item— but it was a treasure that was as precious to me as my life.

One day, I stole a few photos—photos of my mother as a student and as a schoolteacher, photos of my parents' wedding, and a photo of me when I was three years old. However, there are many other photos I remember, ones I do not have anymore—one of the entire family, in which my grandmother is dressed in a fine silk *hanbok*, and some of my father from his college days.

I was afraid that my aunt would get angry, so I did not dare take out any of my father's photos. Decades later, I found out that this package of photos had found its way back to my other aunt who used to live in Seoul but that she had thrown them in the trash years ago.

Another item in that package of photos was a letter from my father to my aunt. My father was most sad to leave me behind, but he promised to come back and find me in three months. He firmly believed that the war would end in the next two months as the North Korean leader Kim Il-sung had promised.

But when a truce in the war was declared, my father never came for me. He never picked me up from my aunt's house, and my aunt eventually tore that letter to pieces and threw into the trash. We had to get rid of or hide anything belonging to my family—anything that linked me to my communist family was dangerous.

It is fortunate that I learned to read before my father's letter was destroyed. I secretly read the letter, and I have thought about my father's promise constantly after first reading it. I waited for my father for a very long time. I did not know then that he had been executed in North Korea in 1956, so I eagerly awaited him, imagining his visit in dreams when my eyes were closed.

My aunt had two older sisters; the oldest was my first aunt and the next youngest was my second aunt (as Koreans, we do not refer to our elders by their first names). One cold winter day, my second aunt suddenly arrived at my aunt's house with her two daughters clothed in rags. They had brought my sickly-looking grandmother who had just returned from Seoul. As soon as she entered the front door, my second aunt wailed and pointed at me. "My precious son left me to follow that girl's father! That bbal-gang-i! That red commie! My son said he is following that girl's family, and now they have gone to North Korea! I do not know if he is alive or dead!" She cried and staggered as if she were fainting.

After my father and my family went to North Korea, my first aunt was caught by the police and detained in jail, in Seoul. My second aunt told us that her sister had been beaten and dragged with shackles on her feet. Then she was thrown out into the street.

My first aunt, who had been a front-runner for a position in the North Korean political apparatus, was eventually sentenced to death by South Korea. Her son, a university student and communist guerrilla fighter, was shot dead by the police in front of the gate at his mother's home.

"We all have been destroyed by that girl's father! Bbal-gang-i! Oh my god! My life is like a dog's life! This rotten, rotten life!"

With each word, my second aunt struggled, pointed at me, and cried. The adults all turned and looked at me, focusing their resentment on me, saying that because of my father's ideology, the precious sons of the family were dead or missing. Their burning looks and words filled my already torn-up heart with bloody tears.

I had nowhere to hide from my father and my family. I was now an abandoned bbal-gang-i child and a war orphan.

Days later, my grandmother, who was very ill, collapsed. For the next few weeks, she lay sick in bed. "My poor granddaughter!" She would constantly call out to me, weeping weakly.

I became a nuisance to everyone as I refused to leave my grandmother's side. I wanted to be next to my grandmother and be with her as she was dying. My beloved grandmother was the only person I could really trust. Sadly, within a month after returning from Seoul, she left me and went to heaven.

It was still wartime. A few of the men in the town bundled up my grandmother's body and placed it into a tiny coffin. They placed it on a small oxcart and brought it into the mountains to bury. My aunt's husband's concubine was standing off to the side, prattling on: "We are in the middle of a war. It is a big production to roll her up in a sheet and squeeze her into a small coffin."

I knew I had to be quiet. I stood there blankly and wept as I watched the small oxcart carry my grandmother's body away until it disappeared in the distance.

***

My grandmother had been a lovely young woman, the only daughter in the household of a Joseon Dynasty military officer. She had a prosperous childhood, but her parents died young, and this began a difficult life for her.

As was customary at that time, after her parents died all her family's property went to her cousin, the first male heir, who her parents had adopted as their son. This cousin claimed my grandmother's parents' estate and left for Tokyo to study. Later, he returned home with his friend Mr. Park, a young man who was also studying abroad. They often came home together during school holidays.

Mr. Park fell in love with my beautiful grandmother and proposed to her. She accepted, and they had three daughters. Because she had only daughters and no sons, my grandmother sat in poor standing with the family. They blamed her inability to bear sons on the fact that her parents died at an early age. Mr. Park soon welcomed a new wife. He also brought a Japanese concubine from Tokyo.

My grandmother, with her three daughters, always desperately wanted a son. She thought if she could just have a son, she might be accepted back into Mr. Park's family.

Then August 29, 1910, happened—the beginning of the Japanese occupation. We call it Gyeongsul Gukchi, which means "Humiliation Day" or "National Disgrace Day." After that day, the Park family went to Manchuria. Mr. Park took his new wife with him and left my grandmother at her home alone with her three daughters.

My mother was the daughter of Mr. Kang, who managed the estate for the Park family after the family had left for Manchuria. My grandmother gave birth to my mother with great difficulty and was disappointed when it was yet again another daughter.

But my grandmother came to rely on my hard-working mother as she would a son, and she lived the rest of her life with our family. Sadly, my father had taken my grandmother's precious daughter and had gone to North Korea.

My poor grandmother lost her parents, her wealth, and her husband. And in the end, because of my father's communist ideology, she lost her precious daughter too. She endured great sorrow and shock.

One day, the gunmen from the anti-communist youth corps knocked on the door of my aunt's house. During the war, in the name of patriotism, several citizen organizations, like the Anti-Communist Youth Corps and the Korean Self-Defense Force, worked to identify and capture anyone with even the smallest connection to the communist North.

They captured not only known communists but anyone who cooperated with communists during the occupation by the North Korean military. They also captured any family members of the accused because, in their minds, they were guilty by association.

So many people belonged to these citizen organizations that many of them took to giving out extra-judicial punishments by simply slaughtering people on the spot. Many people disappeared without a trace, without a voice, without any understanding of why they were being held captive or why they were being put to death. The anti-communist youth would swarm in, gather their "suspects" into one spot, shoot them, and bury them in a pit. War makes people so vicious.

When the North Korean army moved out and the South Korean military came in, many people were killed—though it must be said that the brutality was just as indescribably horrible for many that were captured by the North Korean army.

I lived in anxiety every day because I knew that I was a bbal-gang-i and I committed the sin of having a communist father.

In these terrifying times, when people of the same nation were brutally killing one other, my aunt always told me, "Child, you must breathe quietly, like a baby! That is the only way you will survive. Otherwise, there is no way you will live."

On the day the gunmen from the anti-communist youth corps squad walked into the house and pointed at me, I crouched next to my aunt, who had been sick and was lying down. They told her that they were going to take me. They stared at me with disdain, as if I were a terrible beast or a lowly worm. For them, the only thing to do to a bbal-gang-i was to execute them—no exceptions, not even for a five-year-old girl. I felt a sense of extreme fear.

My aunt raised her sick body and screamed at them.

"What is wrong with you? Yes, her family is communist! But what is the sin of this little child? She is only five years old! This child is innocent! Don't look at her that way! She does not even know what a bbal-gang-i is! This is why we left town and went to the village deep in the mountains to hide. We were not out there working for the North Korean army! If you want to take her, you're going to have to kill me first!"

I stood next to my aunt, who shouted so much that I froze and clung in terror onto the bedlinen on which she was lying. When they finally left, I could feel her trembling like a leaf as she hugged me tightly.

More than seventy years later, I am still haunted by the fear and can sometimes still feel it. Living a life this close to death instilled in me a strong will to survive. I now know how to protect myself like a porcupine.

From that day on, it was forbidden to talk about my family in my aunt's house—not just for me, but for everyone around me. Those taboo items, our family photos and my father's letter, were hidden away deep in my aunt's cabinet. Thus, I pushed away memories of the happy days of our family and kept the memories I needed to survive. And as my survival instinct kicked in, even the good memories faded away, and soon I had only hatred in my heart toward my father.

A Letter to My Father

Dear Father—my red, communist, bbal-gang-i father,

I am writing you now, even though I have spent a lifetime trying not to have this conversation with you.

As I walked the path in North Korea to the place where you were executed, purged by the North Korean government, I wished that I could have had a long conversation with you.

I have missed you so much that it hurts my heart! I have longed to be reunited with you for my entire life! But I have also hated you so much at the same time.

But now I wish to tell you my story, Father. It starts before I was born, on August 15, 1945, Gwangbokjeol, the "Restoration of Light Day," in Korea when our country was liberated from Japan, and it continues to this day, when I am seventy-four years old.

I have lived many lives in that time.

I want to tell you about the founding of the Republic of Korea, about the war that was caused by the ideals you held, and about how painful that tragedy was.

Do you think that your execution in North Korea was the only price that was paid for your sins?

Father, I want you to listen to me. I want you to listen to the little daughter you left behind in Puyo, I want you to hear her story, the story of a little girl who had to live in shame and fear.

I do not know if you were drawn to communism through a romantic nationalism or if you first encountered these ideas when you fled to China to escape Japanese oppression. I do not know when you joined the independence movement or became a member of the Communist Party.

But I want you to know that my life is a byproduct of your actions and your communist ideology.

At the age of four, I could not choose my own direction in life. I have hated you for making that choice for me. I have hated you for the seventy years that I have been separated from my family. Regardless of your intentions, the tragedy of our family began because of your communist ideology.

In seventy years, I have been able to see my mother and brothers in North Korea only one time. Their life and their world were so different from mine, where I had liberalism and freedom.

The reality of our family was tremendously sad and unfortunate. I hated you, Father, throughout my life, but I also have sought to understand you.

I enrolled at the University of Minnesota at the age of thirty-five, where I learned Chinese, modern Chinese history, and Mao Zedong's communist history. The more I learned about this history and ideology, the more I hated the idea of communism. The history of China under Mao Zedong was bloody. It was a history that saw seventy-five million people killed under the Communist Party's terrible dictatorship. I longed for the Communist Party of Mao Zedong and Joseph Stalin to disappear entirely from this earth.

Father, I want to ask you, did you and your Korean intellectual colleagues know how fanatical and ruthless Stalin and Mao were? Did you know how many people those murderers had killed in the name of the Communist Party?

Stalin did not hesitate to call for the murder of his enemies, the destruction of their clans, their families. He sought to execute all who undermined the unity of their communist nation.

You were a member of the Workers' Party of South Korea, and when the war broke out you hurriedly took my mother and brothers and fled to North Korea. I was only four years old, and you left me alone in South Korea.

Everyone pointed at me. "Bbal-gang-i!" It was the day I first felt that bleeding wound in my heart.

Because of your communist ideology, you brought tragedy to our family and relatives. Your little daughter had to survive the pain of every day amid countless wounds and bitter loneliness. You played right into the hands of Stalin, who separated my country, my family. You believed the lies of the Workers' Party's promise of reunification. Your dream, your ideals were a devastating and a disastrous reality for our family and our beloved country.

I have waited for you for a very long time. I did not know that you had already been executed in 1956, purged by the North Korean government. I waited for you long after that. I remember how you would hug me and give me a warm smile. I waited for you in my dreams.

My dearest father, I was so resentful of you and yet so nostalgic for you at the same time. But now I want to rest this wounded heart that has been spending so many years hating you.

You were thirty-six. That was your age when the North Korean government killed you. I have lived two of your lifetimes. So now I want to forgive you by the time I finish writing this book.

Father, Jesus told me to love thy enemies, and yet I have hated you for so long. Every time I pray the Lord's prayer, my heart is always sore. Father, I have not been able to forgive you. I have not been able to live up to the words "forgive us our trespasses as we forgive those who have trespassed against us." May the Lord forgive me as I shed tears of repentance now, as I write these words.

Now I have put down my hatred and decided to love you, my father. Now I will quietly say the Lord's Prayer for you.

Father, it was one late night last year when I received a phone call from Korea. That is when I found out that in 2002, your beloved wife, my mother, had passed away like a hungry beast. Your son, my second brother, also starved to death. In all, five members of our family, including my mother, died of starvation.

Father, it was in the middle of a quiet night when I received that phone call, while everyone was sleeping peacefully. My friend, a North Korean refugee, called to tell me what they had learned about my family—who was dead and who was alive, who had married and who had children. I listened intently as I learned about the family that I had missed so much for so many years. I needed to know the news of this family that I had met only once before in the seventy years of my life.

I hung up the phone with gratitude, and tears poured from my eyes. That night, I revisited that lonely little four-year-old girl, thinking about how for my entire life I have been alone. I let myself go and cried out loud all night long.

Even now, the tears do not stop as I write this.

Father, are you in tears as I am now? Are you hugging me as a father would hug his little daughter? How would we have lived if you had abandoned your ideology and come for me? Since this news, I have been having my family honor their ancestors in the traditional way—for you and for my mother and aunt.

I feel my love for you, Father! And for the Lord who fills my heart day by day.

Father, my dear father, I love you.

I hope you are at peace.

With love,
Your daughter

The Korean War Tragedy

Father, I want you to understand the true history of what happened in our country. I want you to understand the consequences of the decisions of those you chose to follow. I want you to understand the tragedy of the Korean War not just for our family, but for the people of Korea.

China

In the history of the world, China has invaded Korea countless times, treating it like a subordinate nation and harassing its people. Mao Zedong worked with Stalin and Kim Il-sung to cause the Korean War, an action that has kept Korea divided and its people separated for over seventy years.

United States

Relations with the United States began in the mid-nineteenth century with the General Sherman Incident, a failed attempt by the United States to engage in trade with Korea. Diplomatic relations began in 1882 and went until 1905, when Japan took over Korea's international affairs. Relations between the two countries were severed completely in 1910 when Japan annexed Korea. After that, the United States had turned its back on the Korean empire. President Theodore Roosevelt supported the Japanese annexation, negating agreements that the US had made with the Koreans. From that point until the Second World War, this pro-Japanese policy continued.

Japan

In 1910, on our National Day of Disgrace, the Japanese Empire began its brutal occupation of Korea. The occupation went from August 29, 1910, until August 15, 1945. The emperor of Japan controlled Korea through his administrator, the governor-general of Joseon, taking all authority away from the Korean people in political and diplomatic matters. After the unconditional surrender of Japan in 1945, the governor-general of Joseon was removed. This began the period of military occupation, with the United States in the South and the Soviet Union in the North.

Liberation Day

On the morning of August 15, 1945, Emperor Hirohito of Japan announced the surrender of the Japanese army. Koreans took to the streets, cheering, crying, and joyfully waving flags. The Japanese occupation was finally over, and Korea was emerging from the darkness. Korean Liberation Day is known as *Gwangbokjeol,* which literally means "the day the light returned."

Many Koreans had left the country, having been drafted into Japanese military service or having fled to Manchuria after the Japanese forcefully seized their land. Now, as a liberated nation, the hopes and dreams of all Koreans were elevated. Many of those who had left began to return.

But even in the light of a liberated Korea, a dark shadow began to emerge. Our country was divided at the thirty-eighth parallel by two occupying forces, the Soviet troops in the North and the American troops in the South. As the Allied Forces became the victors of World War II, the Japanese Empire was being dismantled. Because Korea had not liberated itself, the Korean peninsula would not yet achieve full independence.

With Soviet forces in the North, Stalin quickly worked to establish communist rule. First, through Kim Il-sung, he conducted land reform in North Korea. They removed all landlords, asset-holders, and major industries, then nationalized all land and property. The Provisional People's Committee of North Korea was formed to govern North Korea, chaired by Kim Il-sung and dominated by communists.

In South Korea, the focus was on elections and reunification. The US occupation ended with general elections to establish the government of the Republic of Korea. Even with Stalin and Kim Il-sung influencing the South Korea Communist Party and seeking to obstruct the election, 96 percent of the South Korean people participated and carried out the vote.

By autumn of 1948, there were two Korean countries on the Korean peninsula with two separate Korean governments. In the South was the Republic of Korea, which respected individual freedom, and in the North was the communist Democratic People's Republic of Korea.

Stalin worked with Kim Il-sung and China's Mao Zedong to try and force South Korea into his dream of a communist Korea. He was very ambitious. North Korea had inherited a huge industrial infrastructure from Japan. Under Stalin's guidance, North Korea built itself into a powerful communist dictatorship.

Meanwhile, in South Korea, Stalin laid the groundwork to make South Korea communist. He strongly supported the actions of communist activist Pak Hon-yong and the Workers' Party of South Korea. He also worked with Kim Il-sung to infiltrate the South.

After its liberation from Japanese occupation, Korea was in a precarious position, standing in between the powerful countries that had fought and won the Second World War. During that war, the United States and the Soviet Union had worked together—after the war, they were in direct conflict. From the moment Stalin showed his desire to make the entire Korean peninsula communist, the United States began to directly confront him.

During this time, a new Korean government began to be established. Exiled Korean politicians and leaders had gathered back in their homeland. In time, what started as ideological divisions became a source of great confrontation between North and South. As these leaders disagreed and fought over the future of Korea, Stalin began pushing North Korea to become more powerful—and become a more fully communist nation. To him, this was the first step in turning the entire Korean peninsula into a communist country.

Stalin worked quickly to occupy the North and make it communist. Before US military forces arrived on the Korean peninsula, a provisional government called the People's Republic of Korea was established on September 6, 1945, working off a network of people's committees that the Soviets had already co-opted in North Korea.

They were looking to focus their political power on ousting any US influence once the US military arrived.

On September 8, 1945, the US military finally arrived in Incheon. The next day, the governor-general of Japan and the Japanese army handed over control of the Korean government in Seoul to the United States. For the next three years, the United States' occupying force, having inherited the administrative bodies and personnel from Japan, operated a military government in South Korea.

Upon his arrival in Seoul on September 9, 1945, US Lieutenant General John Reed Hodge proclaimed that the US military would oversee the South Korean government. On September 16, 1945, the communists openly acknowledged the People's Republic of Korea. Four days later, Stalin issued a secret order to his commander in the Far East with plans for the division of the Korean peninsula.

In October of 1945, Syngman Rhee, a liberal democratic revolutionary, was the first of many Korean activists allowed to return to Korea from the United States. After Rhee's return, many other activists for Korean independence began returning to their home country. By November, many members of the Provisional Government of the Republic of Korea, a Korean government in exile formed in China during the Japanese occupation, began to return. This included Kim Gu, an associate of Syngman Rhee and president of the provisional government.

Syngman Rhee was a liberal revolutionary activist who harbored a deep respect for individual freedom. He was a fierce advocate for a free, independent Korea, enduring imprisonment, torture, and exile for his beliefs. He was a deep political thinker that wrote and published a primer on Korean modernization entitled *The Spirit of Independence*. While living in exile in the United States during the Japanese occupation of Korea, he worked hard to lobby the world for a free, independent, democratic Korea. The US State Department, who had kept tabs on Dr. Rhee's independence activist activities in the United States, tried to prevent his return to Korea. The State Department's concern was that Rhee's strong anti-communist views would hurt negotiations with the Soviet Union on the future of the Korean peninsula. This put Dr. Rhee and the United States government at odds.

Trusteeship

In December of 1945, foreign ministers from the United States, the United Kingdom, and the Soviet Union met in Moscow to discuss postwar issues. This included establishing a joint commission to oversee Korean matters and govern Korea under a trusteeship. According to the Moscow Conference agreement, the United States, the Soviet Union, the United Kingdom, and China would oversee Korea for a period of five years as the Korean people began to create a government and the country rebuilt itself as an independent state.

It had been announced that a US-Soviet joint committee would discuss the future of Korea in consultation with the Provisional Government of the Republic of Korea, which had been formed in exile during the Japanese occupation. A meeting of representatives was scheduled within two weeks to discuss North and South Korea issues.

While the United States, Soviet Union, United Kingdom, and China all supported this approach, many of the Korean people strongly protested because it seemed like a return to occupation and colonization. Syngman Rhee strongly opposed this committee, especially because Stalin was heavily involved in its formation. Kim Gu was also passionately opposed to the committee, launching a powerful campaign to unify the country and oppose the trusteeship.

Professor Park Sung-so, from the Korea Institute of Korean Studies, put it this way: "We thought we had become an independent country, but how could we have independence underneath a trusteeship arrangement? 'Trusteeship' just sounded like another word for 'colony,' thus we opposed it. There was a nationalist backlash against the trusteeship."

Pak Hon-yong, the head of the Communist Party of Korea in the South publicly opposed the idea of a trusteeship the day after it was established on December 28, 1945. After traveling north of the thirty-eighth parallel and consulting with Stalin and his supporters, he reversed his position. On January 2, 1946, he and the Communist Party of Korea voted in favor of the formation of a Soviet-style trusteeship.

Stalin's Korea plan was to follow a strategy that he had employed in Eastern Europe. The Communist Party of Korea joined the coalition regimes, then attempted to oust all other political factions to take complete power of the government. This is the strategy that North Korea's Kim Il-sung and the Communist Party of Korea's Pak Hon-yong followed. By using the same tactics as Stalin had in Eastern Europe, they sought to manipulate the interim coalition government into creating a unified communist Korea.

Kim Il-sung appointed both a minister of the interior and a secretary of defense that gave him total control of the police and the military. He placed supporters in the local people's committees across North Korea, thus they were dominated by communists. He made himself the prime minister and filled the cabinet with his cronies. All of this laid the foundation for a communist government nominally supported by the people but controlled by Kim Il-sung.

South Korea was a different story. Stalin had less influence because there was not the same level of public support for the communists. A strong anti-trusteeship movement existed in the South, even as the North was rapidly transforming into a communist country.

On February 8, 1946, Stalin established the Provisional People's Committee of North Korea and appointed Kim Il-sung as its chairman. This centralized power in North Korea into a single government and allowed Stalin and Kim to implement administrative reforms across the country. In March of 1946, under the direction of Stalin, Kim Il-sung seized any land from all North Korean landowners and redistributed it to over four hundred thousand farmers and households. Around eighty thousand landowners and intellectuals were expelled from their homes as part of this action.

More than ninety thousand members of the rural people's committees had supported the land reform and belonged to the Communist Party of North Korea. These people helped solidify North Korea as a communist state. In the end, they would become leaders in what would become the Workers' Party of North Korea. They remained loyal to Kim Il-sung and survived Kim's purge of many former South Korean communists in 1955 and 1956. Park Hon-yong, the head of the Workers' Party of South Korea, was executed as part of this purge. He was falsely accused and convicted of spying for the United States. The government also began purging Christian leaders and other influential figures, accusing them of being anti-communist. Sadly, this type of governing, through fear and killings, still continues in North Korea today.

As had been planned by Stalin, social reforms were implemented in North Korea, combined with an intense nationalistic push for reunification and loyalty. Also, all important industrial facilities were seized and nationalized by the government.

In August 1946, the Communist Party of North Korea merged with the New People's Party of Korea to establish the Worker's Party of North Korea. This brought the Yan'an, or Chinese faction, into the party. These were Koreans who had been exiled to China and became communists. With multiple factions coming together into a single communist political party, North Korea continued to move toward establishing a totalitarian communist regime. Knowing he could unify and rule the North, Stalin encouraged the US military to establish a unified interim government through a joint committee of the Soviet Union and the United States.

United States – Soviet Union Joint Committee

Winston Churchill's "Iron Curtain" speech of 1946 and the Truman Doctrine of 1947 ushered in the Cold War era. The United States was becoming concerned with the rapid spread of communism after Stalin's successful communist takeover of Eastern Europe.

At the time, there were Communist Party members in the United States and Soviet spies reporting to Stalin. One of President Roosevelt's trusted advisors was Alger Hiss. Hiss had been present at the founding of the United Nations and the conference in Yalta. He was also a Soviet spy working for Stalin.

With his spies in place, Stalin was able to get the jump on the United States in supporting the trusteeship, which he felt would strengthen the Soviet position in North Korea and lead to a unified communist Korean peninsula. With his influence, the first meeting of a US-Soviet joint committee began in March of 1946 at Deoksugung Palace, in Seoul. Stalin had encouraged this idea of a joint committee, but he predictably limited participation to political parties and organizations that supported Moscow.

The United States was aware of Stalin's efforts to strong-arm the committee into exclusively supporting pro-communist groups. The United States, fearing a communist takeover, argued that by the principle of freedom of speech, all major parties and organizations should be allowed to participate, including groups that may oppose the trusteeship and the Moscow Agreement. But the United States also did not want to jeopardize the joint committee talks.

The joint committee met through May of 1946 but found no room for compromise, so it did not come to an agreement. The meetings broke down. Soon after, it was made illegal to cross the thirty-eighth parallel without a permit. Thus, the summer of 1946 saw the beginning of the Cold War era.

A month later, Major General John H. Hildring, the assistant secretary of state overseeing the US-occupied areas, contacted Commander John Reed Hodge, who oversaw the US military government in Korea. He stated that while the United States wanted to allow all parties to freely participate in joint committee talks, the Soviet Union wished to exclude any leaders with a firm anti-Soviet stance, including asylum-seekers like Syngman Rhee and Kim Gu, leaders of the Korean government in exile and the interim government. Because the US saw them as interfering with the US goals for the joint committee, they agreed to exclude them from any talks.

The United States found Syngman Rhee especially problematic because of his strong anti-communist, anti-Soviet stances. This ran counter to the US desire to find compromise with the Soviets on the Korea issue. Even before World War II, Rhee had repeatedly warned the US State Department to be vigilant and not trust the Soviet Union. When he returned to Korea after liberation, he strongly opposed the military occupation of Korea—and also any cooperation between the United States and the Soviet Union.

Had the United States heeded Syngman Rhee's words rather than coming under the influence of Stalin spies like Alger Hiss, the atrocity that was the Korean War may have been avoided.

Instead of Rhee and Kim Gu, Commander Hodge supported more moderate left- and right-wing figures, Yeo Un-hyeong and Kim Kyu-sik, who supported the joint committee. However, by the summer of 1946, the US-supported joint committee with the Soviet Union had failed to find a path to independence for the Korean peninsula.

Syngman Rhee's Proposal

Having been shut out of the joint committee and seeing the talks inevitably break down, Syngman Rhee put forth his own proposal in June 1946. He called out the failure of the joint committee, arguing that an independent Korean government needed to be formed. He recognized that the Soviets had already consolidated power in the North and that any hope for an independent democracy would have to start in the South. While he preferred a unified Korea, he feared a communist Korea more. In his eyes, it was better to establish a successful independent government in the South and use that success as leverage to convince the world that the Soviets should vacate the North.

Rhee returned to the United States from December 1946 to April 1947. He advocated for his plan for Korean independence, lobbying the US State Department to abandon the joint committee with the Soviets. His plan had three primary elements:

1. Hold general elections to establish a South Korean transitional government that would govern until the reunification of the North and South, at which time a new government would be established.

2. Through this transitional government, negotiate directly with the United States and the Soviet Union regarding the end of the military occupation and other vital issues, including reunification.

3. Negotiate war reparations from Japan to help rebuild the Korean economy. (February 12, 1947, *Dong A Daily* newspaper)

However, United States officials continued to work through the US-Soviet joint committee and rejected Rhee's proposal.

Kim Gu, the Anti-trusteeship Movement, and the Communist Party's Plan

Kim Gu continued to campaign against the US and Soviet trusteeship. He sought to establish a Korean government, independent of the US military government.

The Allied forces of World War II had liberated Korea from Japan but divided the peninsula. A communist, pro-Soviet regime was establishing itself in North Korea at lightning speed. Stalin and Kim Il-sung were plotting to reunify the Korean peninsula. It is a tragedy that Kim Gu, a respected leader of the Korean Provisional Government, clashed with Syngman Rhee at such a critical time in history. By July 1946, the Communist Party of Korea, which operated in the South, began organizing demonstrations, sometimes violent, protesting the US military government. The strategy was to pressure the United States and to encourage public support for a unified Korean peninsula under communist rule.

Two months earlier, the party had become embroiled in a counterfeiting scandal. They had been given control of what had been a Jeoson Bank building during the Japanese occupation. They changed its name to Jeong Pan Sa and printed counterfeit money to pay their expenses, which also disrupted South Korea's economy. When they were discovered by the US military, many leaders in the Communist Party were arrested. The official newspaper of the party was also closed by the US military.

In retaliation and as a step toward undermining US military rule, the party declared an all-out public battle with the US military government. This new tactic served to damage the US military government's ability to rule and put public pressure on their withdrawal. The Communist Party of Korea declared a general strike in major cities in September, then staged large-scale protests and uprisings around the city of Daegu. Their strategy served to make South Korea more unstable as the political, social, and economic turmoil intensified.

With the help of Stalin, whose plan was for a reunified communist Korea by the end of 1946, one year after liberation, North Korea organized a terror campaign to solidify the Communist Party in North Korea, to bring leftists in the North and the South in line with the Soviet-sponsored government, and to sow chaos in the South. The actions of the Communist Party undermined Syngman Rhee's efforts to establish a United Nations–sponsored democratic government in the South as it sunk much of South Korea into chaos and lawlessness. Pak Hon-yong and his forces played a particularly significant role in the anti–US military actions and political intimidation tactics.

The United States military's attempts to court the more moderate voices on the left and right eventually failed. And Kim Gu's opposition to the trusteeship meant he was also not an ally to the US. Instead, it was the Stalin-supported faction led by Pak Hon-yong that sparked protest and caused extreme chaos.

Second Meeting of the United States–Soviet Union Joint Committee

The second meeting of the United States–Soviet Union joint committee began on May 21, 1947, and took place in Pyongyang, North Korea. As with the first meeting, Stalin required political parties and social groups to submit a signed document indicating that they support the Moscow Agreement. Once again, he argued that any organizations that had protested the Moscow Agreement trusteeship in any way should not be allowed to participate, even if they signed the pledge.

In the end, the second meeting ended like the first—a complete breakdown in discussions and no agreement. The United States was eager to turn over the government and withdraw their troops from the Korean peninsula. Stalin's interference had ensured that the United States' faith in the Moscow Agreement and the joint committee would not yield results. The United States was determined to find a way to withdraw.

In August, as the second US-Soviet joint committee came to an end, the United States suggested that the Korea issue be discussed in four-party talks between the Moscow Agreement trusteeship nations: the United States, the Soviet Union, Great Britain, and China. The Soviets rejected this idea. In the end, the United States decided to support bringing a resolution to the United Nations.

US Withdrawal, the Korea Issue, and the United Nations

As growing protests and violence put their troops in danger, the United States military wanted to withdraw from Korea as soon as possible. Until this point, the US State Department had resisted, citing the strategic importance of the peninsula. But by September of 1947, there was agreement that the troops should be withdrawn and the United Nations should oversee a transfer of power to the Koreans.

In September 1947, the United States informed the Soviet Union that the issue of Korean self-governance would be brought before the United Nations, then demanded that the UN General Assembly add it to the agenda.

In the same way that their countries shared borders on a map, Stalin, Mao Zedong, and Kim Il-sung, had been working hand in hand with the goal of creating a Communist-controlled, unified Korea.

The decision to withdraw US forces by 1948 was a major mistake and a miscalculation by the United States. It underestimated the roles of North Korea, China, and the Soviet Union in determining Korea's fate.

Had the United States not withdrawn when they did, there may not have ever been a Korean War. This is one decision that could have saved nearly five million lives.

Korea and the UN General Assembly

On September 23, 1947, the United Nations General Assembly officially added Korean independence to its agenda. A subsequent UN resolution created the United Nations Temporary Commission on Korea (UNTCOK). The commission was sent to Korea in January of 1948 to help facilitate and supervise elections on the Korean peninsula.

The Soviets did not recognize the authority of the council, arguing that this broke the agreements at the Moscow Accords, which gave the US, the United Kingdom, the Soviet Union, and China jurisdiction over postwar settlement—and not the United Nations. This meant the UN commission did not have access to North Korea. By February, the UN commission had decided to move forward with elections in South Korea even without North Korea's participation.

An election law passed in March of 1948 declared that Korean National Assembly seats would be proportionally divided based on population. This meant that there would be one hundred North Korean and two hundred South Korean representatives elected. On May 10, 1948, elections were held in South Korea. The explicit goal of the elections and the National Assembly was to rule over a reunified peninsula with North Korean representation. However, Stalin and the Communist Party of North Korea continued to sabotage the process and attempted to undermine the South.

From the beginning, North Korea and the Soviet Union opposed the United States bringing the issue of Korean elections to the United Nations. They hid behind the issue of self-determination, arguing that the Koreans should be left to decide Korean issues. Through this lens, they claimed that the United Nations should not be involved in Korean elections and that US and Soviet troops should withdraw from the peninsula as soon as possible.

But this claim to support Korean interests was merely a ruse for Stalin to achieve his goal of a communist Korean peninsula. The withdrawal of the UN observers and United States troops would have given the North Korean Communist Party the freedom to use the same strong-arm tactics in the South that they used to secure a totalitarian regime in the North.

As in the North, the South Korean communists also had been using violent and vicious tactics, even initiating armed guerrilla strikes. On February 7, 1948, the Workers' Party of South Korea staged a general strike against the UN-sponsored general elections that included bloody clashes with police and attacks on government facilities. On April 3, 1948, another general strike included deadly attacks on police and paramilitary forces. These actions failed in preventing the May 10 election, but they did spark riots that resulted in the tragic deaths of thousands of people.

The communist parties of the North and South were not the only ones fighting to prevent the election. Certain moderate and extreme right-wing factions were also opposed to having separate elections in South Korea without the participation of the North. Kim Kyu-sik and Kim Gu, who, like Syngman Rhee, were influential members of the Korean independence movement dating back to the Japanese occupation, supported an early withdrawal of US and Soviet troops and insisted on negotiations between the North and South on any elections. In April, North Korea and Kim Il-sung invited them and other political leaders to Pyongyang for a conference involving political organizations from the North and South. Syngman Rhee denounced the conference. Kim Kyu-sik and Kim Gu chose to attend and boycott the UN-supported elections in the South. Unsurprisingly, the communist factions did not leave any real room for negotiation or compromise at these meetings. They were just for show.

North Korea used the Pyongyang conference to signal to Korean loyalists that they favored a unified Korea. They sought to manipulate Kim Gu and Kim Kyu-sik by making it seem like this was the only chance to stop the division of the country. On April 19, 1948, they traveled north to the conference. But after days of meetings in which the northern factions asserted their intent to leave room for only a communist government, the single agreement reached by all parties was to denounce the separate general elections in South Korea. A letter sent from Soviet Communist Politburo to Pyongyang one week before the conference confirms that the Soviet Union was behind this strategy.

It is a tragedy that there was so much infighting among those who supported a free, democratic Korean peninsula. If only those disparate voices had united in their efforts to defend the country against Stalin, Kim Il-sung, and the Communist Party, they may have been able to prevent the tragedy that was the Korean War.

Some place the blame on Syngman Rhee and the United States for a divided Korea, but then who would have stopped Stalin and Kim Il-sung from creating a communist Korea? This had been Stalin's goal since 1945, to make Korea communist, like he had in Eastern Europe.

Election Day

May 10, 1948, is one of the most important days in Korean history. On this day, every house in Korea displayed the Korean flag. People dressed in white to line up at their polling places. It was the election day for the first National Assembly of the Republic of Korea. There were 904 candidates, of which 198 were elected to seats in the assembly. Under the watch of United Nations election observers, a free and fair election occurred with a 95.5 percent turnout rate. It was a beautiful sight, a wave of white coming together to claim their sovereignty as a nation.

In these, the first democratic elections in Korea, almost everyone with the right to vote participated in the election regardless of age, gender, or class. Despite the violent protests and public boycotts by communist supporters, the Korean people bravely took to the polls, each of them freely casting their vote for the candidates they truly wanted. With joy in their heart, the Korean people took their first step at reclaiming their independence.

Constitution of the Republic of Korea (South Korea)

On May 31, 1948, the first National Assembly began work on creating the Constitution of the Republic of Korea. Syngman Rhee, the elected speaker, opened the first session: "This National Assembly is a National Assembly to represent all the people of Korea. The government that has been born with the National Assembly is the government that will represent the entire Republic of Korea."

On July 17, 1948, the proposed constitution was made known and presented to the public by the National Assembly. The first article of the constitution stated that the Republic of Korea would be a democratic republic, its sovereignty would reside in the people, and all state authority would emanate from the people.

The Birth of the Republic of Korea

On July 20, 1948, the Korean National Assembly elected Syngman Rhee as the first president of the Republic of Korea with 93 percent of the vote. On August 15, 1948, the constitution went into effect, the Republic of Korea became a country, and Rhee officially became its first president. Three years after the liberation of Korea from the Japanese occupation, Korea had its own government and president.

In the presence of thousands of people, President Rhee proclaimed the establishment of the Korean government. It was a moment nearly forty years in the making—the birth of an independent, free Korea.

On the day of the birth of the Republic of Korea, the Korean people celebrated and shouted, "Long Live Korea!" Thirty-eight years after the Japanese had forcibly taken over Korea in 1910, the long-awaited independent state was reborn as the Republic of Korea. Of course, Stalin and Kim Il-sung made certain that only half of the nation had a truly independent government.

United Nations Approval of the Republic of Korea

On December 12, 1948, the United Nations adopted a resolution recognizing and approving the Republic of Korea's government as the sole legitimate government on the Korean peninsula. As such, the Republic of Korea joined the international community as a legitimately recognized government and independent country.

This laid the groundwork for the United Nations forces to fight alongside the Korean Armed Forces during the Korean War. The South Korean people are deeply grateful to the United Nations forces for saving their nation from the enemy. It is important to remember that having an independent government recognized by the UN is what enabled us to receive much necessary military assistance during the war.

Establishment of the Democratic People's Republic of Korea (North Korea)

Twenty days after the formation of the South Korea, on September 9, 1948, North Korea was also formally established. North Korea had already put together much of this government in April, and it had drafted a constitution that was said to have been personally edited and rewritten by Joseph Stalin and other Soviet supervisors. To avoid appearing responsible for the division of the peninsula, Kim Il-sung, per Stalin's plans, delayed the elections and the proclamation of the Democratic People's Republic of Korea until after the government of South Korea had been established.

But the work had begun back in April. By August, elections were held for the Supreme People's Assembly. Even South Korean communists participated through underground means. On September 3, 1948, a constitution was announced. Government entities such as a cabinet and supreme court were formed. Finally, Kim Il-sung was declared prime minister.

The New South Korea

The Republic of Korea is the first country in the history of the Korean peninsula to place sovereignty in the hands of the people. The fundamental freedom of the individual was ensured. People were able to work and prosper based on their talents. South Korea was born as and still remains a liberal democracy with a market economy.

While Korea had been liberated during World War II, the three years immediately following the war were simply a different kind of occupation, with Soviet troops in the North and US troops in the South. It was the establishment of the Republic of Korea that truly put the Japanese occupation in the past. The fact that this democracy was only established in the South was unfortunate but necessary, given the actions of the Soviets and Kim Il-sung in the North.

The Korean War Plan

Joseph Stalin had succeeded in making Eastern Europe communist. In August of 1945, he dreamed of doing the same with the Korean peninsula. In September of 1948, as soon as the North Korean state was officially established, Stalin and Kim Il-sung began planning to invade South Korea and unify the peninsula under communism by force.

In March of 1949, Kim Il-sung visited the Soviet Union to ask Stalin for permission and support to begin the invasion of South Korea. Stalin suggested postponing the invasion plan to give North Korea time to amass more power and weaponry. He also provided North Korea with weapons, including guns, tanks, and aircraft.

Stalin also instructed Kim to consult China's Mao Zedong on the invasion plan. Then Kim Il-sung sent a North Korean representative to China at the end of April 1949 to inform Mao Zedong of his alliance with Stalin and his plans to invade South Korea. Mao also suggested waiting to invade and gathering more power. He sent two divisions of the People's Liberation Army of China to Kim Il-sung to help North Korea prepare for war.

Unfortunately, as North Korea and the Soviets were amassing power, beginning in September of 1948 the United States became war-weary and begin reducing their troop presence in Korea. In April 1949, a full-scale withdrawal began—and by May 28, forty-five thousand soldiers had been withdrawn, leaving only five hundred military advisers.

After the withdrawal of the US forces in June, Kim Il-sung went back to Moscow in August to seek permission from Stalin to invade the South. Stalin continued to be cautious, not wanting to start the invasion before there were enough forces in place. Instead, he encouraged South Korea communist guerrilla fighters to use their powers against the South Korean government. In September, they did just that, launching a significant offensive against police stations, government offices, and military depots in cities across South Korea.

In August of 1949, a successful test of an atomic bomb meant that Stalin's aspirations to become a nuclear power were finally fulfilled. This was his established prerequisite before openly engaging the United States in Korea.

Then, in October, Mao Zedong, with Stalin's support, successfully won the civil war for the communists in China. Kim Il-sung was encouraged by the fact that the United States had chosen not to intervene in China. To him, this meant that they would also not intervene when he invaded South Korea.

In January of 1950, Kim Il-sung contacted Stalin through an ambassador, hoping to schedule talks about the invasion of South Korea. Stalin responded by emphasizing how enormous of an undertaking this invasion would be and that they required large-scale preparations. However, Stalin agreed to have a dialogue with Kim if he felt he was prepared.

In early April of 1950, Kim Il-sung and Park Hun-young, a North Korean foreign minister, visited Moscow to discuss the invasion. During these talks, Stalin agreed to support North Korea in a war with South Korea for communist reunification, on the condition that China also agreed to provide support. This was spelled out in a top-secret missive sent from Stalin to Mao Zedong a few weeks later. Stalin wanted to include China to make it clear to the world that the Soviet Union was not unilaterally driving this war.

Mao Zedong was more interested in a communist Taiwan than he was in a communist South Korea. However, he was in no position to oppose Stalin because China still needed the economic and military support of the Soviet Union. Mao decided to support Kim Il-sung and his invasion of South Korea.

In the time after US forces had withdrawn from South Korea in May of 1949, Stalin had been preparing with Kim Il-sung and Mao Zedong to wage a war to conquer the Korean peninsula and make it communist. An ominous storm was brewing that threatened the new Republic of Korea.

Kim Il-sung, with the support of Stalin and Soviet military advisers, planned a preemptive strike on South Korea. His intent was to take the South quickly by using overwhelming force. As Professor Kim Young-ho at Sungshin Women's University has stated, "If you look at the North Korean preemptive strike plan where first they take Seoul, then Daejeon, then Busan, it was written in Russian. It is a certainty that Soviet military advisers were deeply involved in planning the invasion of South Korea."

The Korean War: 1,129 Days, from June 25, 1950, to July 27, 1953

In June of 1950, Stalin approved the date of the invasion of South Korea. It was June 25, 1950. The biggest concern of Stalin, Kim Il-sung, and Mao Zedong was the possibility that the United States would engage in the war. To lessen the chance of this occurring, their strategy was to end the war quickly—within two months. Their reasoning was that this would not give the United States time to respond, and the war would be completed before the US military ever arrived on the Korean peninsula.

The United States was unaware of these plans. The US had even placed weapons restrictions on the South Korean military for fear that they may instigate a military action to reunite the peninsula from the

South. The US also made a tragic miscalculation by assuming that the Soviet Union would not try to invade South Korea for at least five years. As a result, the conditions were favorable for North Korea's invasion—and the Republic of Korea was unprepared for war. This attack was bound to be disastrous for South Korea.

At 4:00 a.m. on Sunday, June 25, 1950, the North Korean military crossed the thirty-eighth parallel and began a preemptive invasion of South Korea. The attack was launched all along the thirty-eight parallel in border areas and cities such as the Ongjin Peninsula, Dongducheon, Pocheon, Chuncheon, and Jumunjin. North Korean warships also landed south of Gangneung in Jeongdongjin and Jumunjin. At 1:35 p.m., Kim Il-sung made an announcement on a North Korean broadcasting service that South Korea had rejected North Korea's proposal for peaceful reunification and had attacked North Korea at the Ongjin Peninsula. This was a lie designed to cover up the fact that North Korea had conducted an unprovoked, preemptive strike against South Korea.

Unfortunately, the South Korean military was not equipped to stop an attack by a North Korean military force. The North Korean military had twice as many soldiers as South Korea, along with hundreds of Soviet-made aircraft and tanks. On that first day of the war, the North Korean military immediately began marching toward Seoul, sending some forces through Gaesong and Munsan but concentrating its main force in the Uijeongbu corridor.

Once the North Korean military had reached Seoul, the attacking force had nearly seven times the artillery power of its opponent. The South Korean military even started sending rear-stationed forces to the front lines, but it was insufficient. By the morning of June 28, the North Korean forces had crossed the final defensive line at Miari and captured Seoul. The South Korean troops were unprepared, outnumbered, and facing an experienced Chinese Korean army that had fought in the Chinese Civil War.

Despite their inexperience and smaller numbers, the South Korean Armed Forces fought bravely against the North Korean army, risking their lives against difficult odds. The South Korean soldiers were more tenacious and less likely to surrender than some of the divisions the Chinese Korean forces had encountered during the Chinese Civil War. The South Korean Sixth Infantry and South Korean civilians were even able to thwart initial attacks on Chuncheon.

The Sixth Infantry Division of the South Korean army fought hard against the second division of the North Korean army and was able to delay their march on Seoul by three days.

As the North Koreans approached, President Syngman Rhee and his cabinet fled Seoul. The government of the Republic of Korea and the president needed to survive this North Korean invasion. However, that same government failed to adequately inform the citizens of Seoul to do the same. Had there been better communication, not as many residents would have been stuck in Seoul during the North Korean occupation.

Syngman Rhee fled Seoul at 3:00 a.m. on June 27, 1950, with members of his cabinet and the National Assembly. At 2:00 a.m. on June 28, the South Korean army detonated the Hangang Bridge over the Han River to delay the invasion of the North Korean army into the rest of South Korea. With no official word to evacuate coming over the government-sponsored radio broadcasts, most of the residents of Seoul did not get out.

North Korean troops entered Seoul on June 28, 1950. Most of Seoul's nine hundred thousand residents were left behind enemy lines. They endured the uncertainty and the difficult conditions of living under the North Korean occupation until Seoul was retaken by the South three months later.

As North Korean forces continued to advance, the government temporarily moved its headquarters to Daejeon, then further south to Daegu, and finally down to the southeastern coastal city of Busan.

The North Korean flag was flying over Seoul, which was now occupied by Kim Il-sung's troops. It had taken three days for the North Korean forces to overcome the tenacious but outnumbered South Korean troops and capture Seoul north of the Han River. These three days gave the South Korean army time to regroup and prepare for up-coming battles. Even more importantly, it gave time for the United Nations to become involved and commit troops to the conflict.

On the morning of June 25, 1950, when President Syngman Rhee heard the report of the North Korean invasion, he stated that he welcomed the support of the UN and democratic allies in this conflict and hoped it could help solve the "Korea problem" or reunify the country as a democratic state. He also warned that every effort must be made to avoid making Korea a "second Sarajevo."

The assassination of Franz Ferdinand in Sarajevo is often seen as the spark that ignited the First World War, which killed tens of millions of people. Rhee recognized that North Korea's actions could have a similar effect and bring the world powers into direct conflict. Kim Il-sung's action was a direct Soviet-supported communist attack on a capitalist democracy. The United States and the United Nations would inevitably strike back.

Help from the United States and the United Nations

On June 24, the US Secretary of State reported to President Truman that the North Korean military had crossed the thirty-eighth parallel and invaded South Korea. President Truman was furious and vowed to stop North Korea at any cost. He felt that ceding control of the Korean peninsula to the communists would cause instability in the region. Truman immediately called for a meeting of the United Nations Security Council, where he demanded a quick resolution to this issue.

On June 25, 1950, the UN Security Council declared North Korea's invasion an act of aggression and demanded they withdraw their forces. Joseph Stalin and Kim Il-sung ignored this order. On June 27, the UN passed a resolution to send troops to defend South Korea, only two days after the North Korean invasion. It is important to note that the quickness of this response is largely because South Korea was formed under a UN resolution and thus was a UN member nation. An attack on a UN member nation by an unrecognized nation is an attack on the United Nations itself.

In early July, a command structure was formed, and General MacArthur was appointed commander of the United Nations Armed Forces. Because the act of aggression had come from communist forces under Stalin and Kim Il-sung, many countries were willing to support the war effort.

In total, twenty-one UN countries provided personnel during the Korean War, with sixteen nations providing troops, and the other five, medical assistance. A total of fifty-nine countries supported South Korea with either monetary aid or personnel. During the Korean War, there were approximately 1.1 million Korean armed forces members, 630,000 UN troops, and over 3,000 medical personnel. Five nations provided mobile surgery units, hospital ships, and field hospitals. Thirty-eight countries provided nearly $8 million in financial aid. This was a shining moment for the United Nations in that members showed real commitment to the preservation of democracy in South Korea.

As for the United States, they began deploying naval and air force units to Korea from Japan on June 26, one day after the invasion. By June 29, General MacArthur was inspecting the front-line troops in Yeongdeungpo, an area of Seoul just south of the Han River. He was also seeking ways to stop the North Korean military's advance into the south.

On July 19, 1950, President Truman addressed the citizens of the United States on radio and television: "What is happening now in a small country thousands of miles away is essential to all Americans. The fact that communists invaded Korea is a warning that similar attacks will be conducted elsewhere." President Truman recognized that Stalin was the root cause of this war. Truman was an early believer in the domino theory of geopolitics, and worried that if Korea fell, Stalin would push his military and his communist influence into other parts of the world.

The Han River was the first line of defense. Further south, near Daejeon, the Geum River formed the secondary line. And finally, the Nakdong River north of Daegu and Busan was the third and final line of defense. The South Korean military developed a strategy of drawing

North Korean troops deep into South Korea, then counterattacking them. The North Korean military eventually broke through the first line of defense at the Han River and the second line at the Geum River. They then pushed on to the Nakdong River, the final line of defense.

Two months into the war, the UN and South Korean forces had been pushed back to the Nakdong River and held an area comprised of only ten percent of South Korea. Most of the peninsula was now being held by the North Korean military.

From the beginning of August into mid-September, the two sides continued to battle at the Nakdong River, South Korea's final line of defense. The US military, which had complete control over the air, launched an onslaught against the North Korean military. With this air support, the ground troops were able to stop the advance of the North Koreans.

Just north of Daegu, in a region called Dabudong, a fierce, fifty-five-day battle ensued. Tactical positions were taken and retaken multiple times during this period. In the end, it was a significant, hard-fought victory for the South. Losses on both sides were massive, with the North Koreans suffering twenty-two thousand casualties and the South Korean and UN troops losing ten thousand. It became difficult at times to even maintain enough forces to sustain the battle. New recruits were often sent to the front lines with only hours of training. Schoolchildren who had never before handled a weapon were dying on the battlefield in large numbers.

This war was a terrible war for the South Korean people. While North Korean forces occupied most of the Korean peninsula, many civilians suffered and died. Additionally, the North Korean military often conscripted troops from the occupied areas. So many South Korean young men were separated or even forcibly abducted from their families and then died in battle.

This war was a war in which brothers and sisters fought and killed one another in their homeland. It was the war of Stalin, of communist oppression. And it was a war in which South Korea seemed hopelessly outnumbered. For every South Korean soldier, the North Korean army had four. The South did not have the manpower nor the equipment nor the weaponry to adequately defend itself against the North Korean military and their Soviet tanks. Yet the outnumbered, inexperienced South Korean forces continued to fight.

Incheon Landing Operations

On September 15, 1950, the United Nations forces, led by General MacArthur, launched an operation to land in Incheon, a port on the western coast north of Seoul. This move put the landing UN troops in the position to block any retreat by the North Korean forces into the central part of the Korean peninsula. This landing coincided with a plan to launch a major counterattack on the Nakdong River front, which would push the communist forces north, toward the troops landing in Incheon. It was a historic turning point in the war.

September 28 – The Restoration of Seoul

The landing of the MacArthur-led United Nations forces in Incheon completely changed the course of the war. On September 28, 1950, the United Nations troops and South Korean Armed Forces recaptured Seoul. The question now was whether to cross the thirty-eighth parallel and make a move toward North Korea.

President Rhee argued that the North Korean invasion had nullified any agreement regarding the border at the thirty-eighth parallel. Rhee felt that this was the opportunity to drive the North Korean regime off the Korean peninsula for good. After convening a meeting with the Korean army commanders at the headquarters in Daegu in September of 1950, he issued an order for South Korean forces to push past the thirty-eighth parallel into North Korea.

He pushed for the South Korean military to cross the border, but he also understood that if UN forces crossed into North Korea, it could trigger a new world war. He argued for unilateral action by the South Koreans. On October 1, 1950, South Korean troops crossed into North Korea.

Then, six days later, on October 7, 1950, UN forces also crossed the thirty-eighth parallel into North Korea with approval from the UN General Assembly. It had been a fierce debate within the UN. Many feared that an invasion of North Korea could escalate the war by causing China and the Soviet Union to commit additional troops. Others argued, as Rhee did, that the North Korea had violated the thirty-eighth parallel agreement. Thus the best course going forward was to push north and ideally eradicate any Soviet and Chinese influence from the Korean peninsula.

By October 19, the first division of the South Korean Armed Forces entered the North Korean capital city of Pyongyang.

That month, the leader of the Sixth Division of the South Korean Armed Forces reached the Yalu River (also known as the Amrok River) along the border of North Korea and China. The UN military forces were engaged in a final offensive to drive the communists out of the Korean peninsula. Everyone thought the war was nearing its end. Kim Il-sung was now in a desperate situation.

On October 1, when South Korean troops first crossed the border, Kim Il-sung and Park Hun-young sent a telegram to Mao Zedong and Stalin, asking them for assistance. They explained that North Korea would not be able to overcome this crisis with the forces they had and that they were in dire need of additional military support from China.

On October 12, Kim Il-sung secretly left Pyongyang and moved farther north to a city called Tokchon. By October 19, he had moved to a backcountry region near the Chinese border. Then, to escape the US forces bombardment near the east coast, he moved to an area in North Pyongan Province, in the farthest northwestern corner of the country. His dream of a reunified, communist Korea was lost. Now he could only hope for the intervention of China and the Soviet Union to at least preserve what he had built in North Korea.

The Soviet Union and China eventually decided to commit more resources to the war. Mao Zedong sent troops as promised, saying, "If North Korea is destroyed, China is exposed, just as not having lips would make your teeth grow cold." China sent the so-called People's Volunteer Army to assist North Korea. Now the Chinese communist soldiers were overwhelmingly involved in the war. On October 19, 1950, under Commander Peng Dehuai, about three hundred thousand troops began to enter North Korea through three different crossing points along the Yalu River.

Now Chinese soldiers were the dominant force for the communist army. The Chinese military also took de facto control of all North Korean military operations. The People's Volunteer Army of China was a formidable force, having fought the Japanese as well as Chiang Kai-shek.

The Soviet Union also intervened more strongly, deploying their air force in November of 1950. However, out of a concern that their involvement would escalate the United States commitment to the war, Stalin took steps to disguise the Soviet forces. The pilots wore Chinese uniforms and the aircraft had Chinese and North Korean markings. Pilots were also instructed to speak only Chinese if they were ever captured by the enemy.

Rather than immediately go on the offensive, the Chinese forces waited for the United Nations and South Korean troops to advance toward the Chinese border in North Korea. Then on November 1, 1950, they launched an attack in the northwest town of Unsan. The UN and South Korean forces were not prepared for the sheer number of Chinese troops—and experienced a high number of casualties. Similar outcomes happened in other North Korean regions like Unsan and the Chosin Reservoir. Despite hearing statements confirming large troop numbers as told by captured Chinese soldiers, the UN forces underestimated the strength of the Chinese army.

The final attack launched by UN forces was the so-called Home by Christmas offensive which begun on November 24, 1950. The Chinese army was waiting in ambush, outnumbering UN forces six to one. This was another significant loss, and the UN forces began to retreat south.

The UN forces in the northeast also encountered a considerable number of Chinese divisions. Looking to take over North Korea's temporary capital in Kanggye, UN troops entered a region near the Chosin Reservoir on November 27, 1950. There they were besieged by an overwhelming force of 120,000 Chinese troops that surrounded them. UN forces were outnumbered four to one and fought a brutal battle for fifteen days in bitterly cold temperatures as low as negative thirty-five degrees Fahrenheit. US forces suffered some of the worst levels of casualties in their history. In the end, UN forces still inflicted heavy casualties on Chinese forces. They thwarted the immediate advancement of the Chinese army and successfully broke through to Hungnam, a port city on the east coast where they were evacuated.

At Hungnam, an evacuation of historic proportions was executed by the UN forces. Over a period of nine days nearly two hundred shiploads of troops and equipment were transported safely to South Korea. This included one hundred thousand North Korean civilians seeking freedom from the communist North. This event is sometimes referred to as the "Miracle of Christmas."

January Fourth Retreat

The Chinese and North Korean militaries launched a New Year's offensive into South Korea in January of 1951. By January 4, the UN and South Korean forces had retreated out of Seoul, and for the second time during the Korean War, the capital city was lost.

However, by March 15 the United Nations forces had reclaimed Seoul, and by the middle of April, the so-called Kansas Line, a UN-defined line slightly north of the thirty-eight parallel, was established as a border. This would eventually become the modern border between North and South Korea. A series of military operations were carried out by both sides in April and May. Then it became clear that neither side would be able to gain significant ground through force. A truce was required. Discussions of an armistice agreement began on July 10, 1951.

Armistice Agreement

Though armistice discussions began in 1951, an agreement was not reached until 1953. The United States and the Soviet Union agreed in principle that there must be a truce. The primary elements that needed to be resolved for a truce to occur were the establishment of a border between the North and South and the exchange of prisoners. Both sides agreed on using the Kansas Line between the opposing armies rather than the thirty-eighth parallel for the border.

The issue of prisoners of war was contested more strongly and was the primary reason for the drawn-out negotiations. Some of the UN prisoners of war had no interest in returning to North Korea or China. The United Nations favored allowing the prisoners to decide their own fate, but the communist sides disagreed with this approach. This point stalled the armistice talks for some time. However, in the end, the United States, the Soviet Union, and China all wanted a ceasefire. In March of 1953, armistice talks reopened.

From this point on, President Syngman Rhee's strong opposition to the truce began. President Rhee opposed the armistice because he feared it would codify the division of Korea and spell the end of any reunification plan for the Republic of Korea. In the end, he withdrew the Republic of Korea army from any armistice talks. He also threatened to have South Korea unilaterally continue the war even if a ceasefire was signed by all other parties.

But President Rhee's opposition to the armistice talks also had another purpose. Rhee feared any ceasefire that did not include a security guarantee from the United States. If the US forces withdrew after the armistice, South Korea would once again be under threat of unprovoked aggression from North Korea—backed by the Soviet Union and China.

In 1952, President Truman asked his generals to develop a contingency plan to overthrow Syngman Rhee if he undermined negotiations to end the Korean War. It was called Operation Eveready. By June of 1953, the Eisenhower administration gave serious consideration to implementing the plan. However, in the end, the United States decided to negotiate a security pact with South Korea to avoid continued retaliatory actions from Rhee.

On June 18, 1953, President Rhee released twenty-seven thousand North Korean prisoners of war with anti-communist views. He did this as a clever political move, knowing it would undermine armistice negotiations. He wanted a promise from the United States that there would be no armistice without a security agreement that protected South Korea. This action astonished the United States, which initially threatened to withdraw their troops entirely. However, cooler heads prevailed and Rhee's demands for a mutual defense agreement began to be taken seriously.

In July of 1953, President Eisenhower sent Assistant Secretary of State for Far Eastern Affairs Walter S. Robinson as a special envoy to convince President Rhee to support the Korean War armistice terms. He assured Rhee that the United States would sign a mutual defense treaty with the Republic of Korea. Since this was Rhee's primary demand, he issued an official statement with Mr. Robinson in support of the ceasefire, promising to cooperate with the upcoming peace treaty negotiations at the Geneva Conference in May 1954 as established in the terms of the armistice.

The armistice negotiations were also helped by the death of Stalin on March 5, 1953. This accelerated negotiations as the new Soviet leadership wanted a quick end to the war, and thus Mao Zedong felt less supported in his unwillingness to compromise.

On July 27, 1953, at 10:00 a.m., the Korean Armistice Agreement was signed at Panmunjom, a village on the border of North and South Korea. It was signed by representatives of the United Nations forces, the Chinese army, and the North Korean military.

After three years, one month, and two days, the war finally entered a truce. However, the Korean War had already taken its toll on North and South Korea, and both suffered profound physical and human damage.

The Cost of War

South Korea

- South Korean military casualties: 620,000
- South Korean civilian casualties: 990,000
- United Nations military casualties: 150,000
- Families divided: 10 million
- War orphans and widows: hundreds of thousands
- Destruction of infrastructure, schools, public facilities, roads, railways, bridges, institutional facilities, factories, and industrial facilities

North Korea

- North Korean military casualties: 640,000
- Chinese military casualties: 970,000
- North Korean civilian casualties: 1.5 million
- Destruction of industrial facilities, houses, buildings, and institutional facilities (many of which were superior to those in South Korea at that time)

When combined to include South Koreans, North Koreans, Chinese soldiers, and United Nations soldiers, 4.87 million people were killed, lost, or wounded in the Korean War. The war produced hundreds of thousands of war orphans and widows and separated ten million families.

So many people were killed in this war conceived by Joseph Stalin and Kim Il-sung—in this attempt to forcibly reunify the Korea peninsula under a communist regime. It was a devastating event for the Korean people.

On the other hand, the Korean War helped shape the national consciousness of the Republic of Korea. In the summer of 1950, South Koreans who were forced to experience communist rule desperately realized the importance of a liberal democracy. This experience remained in their consciousness and inspired a patriotic pride in the citizens of the Republic of Korea.

Kim Il-sung purged any critics within his country that accused him of causing the war. He declared himself a deity, justifying this as part of his imposed North Korean ideology of *Juche*, or self-reliance. North Korean communist groups kidnapped about 200,000 young South Korean people into the People's Army of North Korea and marched most of them into certain death. As the number of people kidnapped or killed became exposed, it seemed impossible to comprehend the North Koreans' limitless cruelty.

North Korea's rural areas re-implemented agricultural reforms that had been established before the war, but there was no benefit to farmers. Instead, in exchange for handing out the land, the government collected taxes in kind, putting a significant burden on farmers.

The fear people experienced during such a tragic war and under such a repressive leader does not easily dissipate. Instead, it drills deep into people's souls. Fearful people can do things that are devilish and terrible. They can accuse each other of terrible things. The North Korean government required citizens to attend daily civil service classes and rallies. Thousands of people were tried and executed as traitors. People were encouraged to accuse family and friends. People became extremely weary and desperate.

North Korea's one-party, Stalinist, communist dictatorship was very harsh. In the hearts of South Koreans who have experienced a liberal democracy as compared to the short period under North Korean rule, there is little doubt which option is preferred.

Once the Korean War armistice was in place, the United States fulfilled its promise to President Rhee and signed a mutual defense treaty with the Republic of Korea, ensuring that the US would continue to protect South Korea from North Korean attacks. It was signed on October 1, 1953, and went into effect on November 17, 1954.

In the end, the Korean War, which had begun on June 25, 1950, ended in a truce, leaving a bloody legacy of tragedy and death in its wake. It resulted in hundreds of thousands of war orphans and widows and ten million divided families. It also resulted in a divided Korea and a heavily armed border with more than one million landmines.

Wedding of Hyon Kim's mother and father *(date unknown)*,
Church courtyard, Seoul
Credit: Photo Collection of Hyon Kim

The aunt who raised Hyon Kim from the age of four years
(June 1950 – May 1963)
Credit: Photo Collection of Hyon Kim

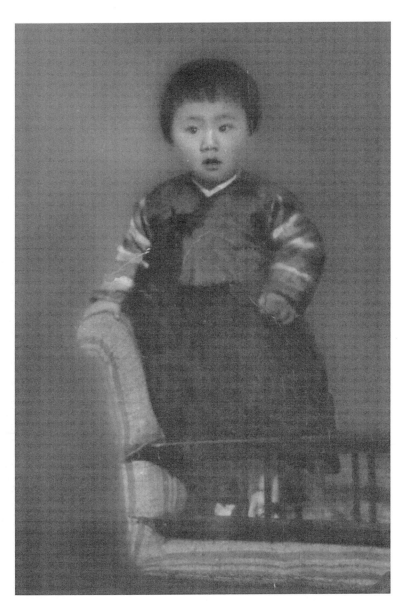

Hyon Kim at the age of two years, 1948, Seoul
Credit: Photo Collection of Hyon Kim

Hyon Kim's mother and father *(date unknown)*
Credit: Photo Collection of Hyon Kim

CHAPTER TWO

The Korean people suffered greatly amid the destruction, death, pain, and chaos of war. This hellish war did not end quickly but instead dragged on, with North and South Korea pushing and pulling each other at the thirty-eighth parallel.

In the middle of this seemingly never-ending war, I was all alone. From the time I was four until I was seven years old, I lived in the battlefield without my family.

Around ten million families became separated during the war. My family was one of them. The land of this war-torn Korean peninsula was covered in blood and now suffered from extreme poverty.

In rural areas, vast swaths of the countryside were full of people who struggled every day with nothing to eat. The Korean word for famine is *bori-gogae*, which means "barley hill." We had no rice, and the barley crop would not be ready for many months, so the famine was like a barren hill we had to climb before we could harvest the barley.

In the city's slums, people lived in rickety shacks made of planks of wood. Entering these slums was like walking through a jungle.

After the truce, the police station, post office, schools, and government offices in the rural town where I lived began to open, and life began to normalize.

I was old enough to start attending school. My aunt officially registered me as her eldest daughter despite her husband's objections. In essence, she was adopting me. By doing so, she was able to erase the link to my family's communist history.

At the time, it was common to create an amended family record because there were many families who had no way of finding each other after being separated during the war. If my aunt had not saved me by making this change to her family record, it would have been difficult for me to survive. I would not have been able to go to school or join the military or immigrate to the United States of America.

It was not only devastating that my family had gone to North Korea; it could have been deadly. At that time, if a South Korean family fled to North Korea, those who were left behind could be killed.

In 1990, I went to North Korea to meet my family for the first time in forty years. My mother and my family members in North Korea had all assumed that I had been killed. Or if I had somehow stayed alive, they thought I would have become a prostitute.

I am grateful for the wisdom and kindness of my aunt in saving me from such an awful situation. I also am thankful to God, who I feel has always protected me.

I finally was able to enter elementary school. Even in the midst of all this tragedy, I enjoyed attending school. I studied very hard and was always top of my class. I was also the class leader.

My aunt lived in a large, spacious house in the countryside. Ours was a nice house that had been confiscated from the Japanese after the occupation ended. My aunt's husband had farmland and hired field hands to work the crops. He also owned an iron shop and sold bicycles. He had a few employees, and business was doing well. I remember he would spend every night stacking and counting the money he earned that day.

He also had a gambling habit and took on mistresses. Despite this, and even though we lived out in the countryside, living at my aunt's house was a life without want. There was never a shortage of anything.

However, I was still a four-year-old child who was suddenly abandoned by her family to live in the countryside, then lost her grandmother. I was also growing up in a household that did not want me at all—and it was not an easy life.

My aunt's husband, the owner of the house, never acknowledged me and was always disgusted by me. I lived there for eleven years, and he never spoke a word to me in that entire time. He was always annoyed by me and avoided me. He hated me because my father was a bbal-gang-i and because my family fled to North Korea.

He especially complained about my aunt officially registering me as a child under his name. He forbade me to call him father, not that I would have ever wanted to do so, thus we never spoke, not directly. If he had a question regarding me, he always asked my aunt. He was good at making money—a good provider, I suppose—but he was an ignorant, savage man who had six mistresses in his lifetime.

When I think about it, I do not even remember ever calling him uncle. I have no memory of ever enjoying my time with him. Yet somehow, I lived in the same house with this man for eleven years.

Even though my aunt had saved me, she was also a very cold person, especially to me. Maybe it was because her life was most difficult. Sadly, when I was being troublesome or bothered her, she would beat me relentlessly. Sometimes she caught my head in her hands and would rip out my hair by the handful. When she talked to her friends about me, I was an annoyance, just her poor niece, a pesky child.

She put my name in her family record, but she did not see me as her child. My aunt was doing this for my mother, whom she loved dearly and who eventually died in North Korea. My aunt and my mother had different fathers, but she thought of my mother as a sister, a younger sister whom she loved and admired.

My aunt had kicked me out of her house when I was sixteen, but years later I then took care of her from the time I was nineteen years old. I also brought her to the United States and looked after her for forty-six years until she passed away at ninety-five-years old. The last thirteen years of those years, she had Alzheimer's disease. After everything, I am truly her only daughter.

The village near Puyo where I lived had an open market every five days. Seoul did not have this kind of market. On market days, the whole town was bustling and lively. One of the more exciting attractions was the medicine-man show. He would demonstrate all sorts of strange, exciting things and do a funny act. He would always draw a large crowd of onlookers that would burst out in laughter and applause that you could hear from far away. There would also be stands with delicious noodle soups boiling away in big cauldrons. All kinds of delicious food would fill the market, and everything smelled good. Many exciting things were there, and I loved them all. It easily took half the day to see and experience everything.

On market days, it was also busy at my aunt's house. My aunt's husband's relatives and my aunt's friends would come to the market and then drop by the house. It made the house very crowded. When all these people would enter the house, they would act like they did not know me. And while they waited for my aunt to bring food from the kitchen, they would talk about me.

The relatives of my aunt's husband would gossip about my aunt and how she was unable to have a child. They would say, "How dare she bring that girl into that house, that bbal-gang-i! Red! Commie!"

When my aunt's friends stopped by, with a distressed look my aunt would lament about having to share a house with her husband's concubine and how she had no children of her own. She would remonstrate and cry, and I knew it was because she did not see me as her child. It made me most sad.

It became a painful ritual, so by the end of every market day, I always wanted to go back to my home in Seoul and be with my family. I wanted to see my father, my mother, and my brothers. I wanted to see the small gate to my house. I would often dream about my father coming to get me.

As I remember these things now, I would like to tell all adults that no matter how young children are, they understand the things the adults are saying to each other, more than you realize. Adults should refrain from saying things that might be hurtful to the children that are listening. Sometimes an adult's careless words can hurt so much that they make a child's heart bleed.

These deep wounds that I received as a child had a significant impact on my relationships and marriages throughout my life.

My father loved me but abandoned me. My aunt's husband was always hostile or indifferent to me. And he was abusive to my aunt.

These behaviors imprinted on me experiences that have hurt me all my life. The men in my life have been just like my father and my aunt's husband.

As a child, I waited for a long time for my father's return after he left me in Puyo at my aunt's house. Eventually, I became exhausted from the waiting—and started hating him instead.

Feeling like Cinderella and waiting for a prince to save me had always been my dream, but when it came time to choose a man, there were never any princes. I always ended up choosing someone like my father or my aunt's husband.

For much of the rest of my life, I have lived by myself, trying to take care of myself and my two sons. I always felt very lonely. And I never received material or mental support from any man. Instead, I supported my husband and raised my children. I do not know why I continued to wait my entire life for a prince and not give up the fantasy. Who would come to save me in my Cinderella story?

In the village where I lived, after more than three years of the horrible war, the weddings that had been postponed started to occur. I had become known in the rural town where I lived as the "cute pale-skinned girl from Seoul." I did get a lot of attention from the village and the church.

Many of the village people with upcoming weddings asked my aunt if I would be their flower girl. As the flower girl, I would hold a flower basket, process in front of the bride, and gently sprinkle flower petals in her path. It was an exciting thing for me to be a flower girl at all those wedding ceremonies.

Usually, the wedding ceremony was held at the village church or in a Buddhist temple far away from the village. It was great fun riding in a big rental car and going to the temple with many people. I was often as happy and excited as the bride.

The brides were always very nice and beautiful. They would give me compliments, and the whole congregation would comment about how cute I was. I would wear a pink *hanbok*, a traditional Korean dress, while I held my basket of flowers and sprinkled petals in the bride's path.

The bride, who hid her beautiful face behind a veil, would shyly turn to the groom as she stepped on the petals and floated down the aisle like an angel. Everyone at the wedding was happy, and I was able to eat a lot of delicious food.

Even though my aunt would send me to these weddings, she was always annoyed by the request. When people asked her if I would be their flower girl, she always bluntly remarked, "She can't be a wedding flower girl. Why would you want her to be your flower girl? This girl is not from a happy family. Why can't you find someone from another house with a proper family?"

She would say these things as if I could not hear her. I was sad and deeply hurt when my aunt said something like that in front of me, pretending as if I did not understand her. She always said to me, "You need to be a quiet, less-outgoing child." I could never say anything because I felt like I had done something wrong.

Still, they kept asking my aunt if I would be their flower girl, and she would reluctantly allow it. The same was true at church and at school. I could always hear her instructions to stay quiet, to be more submissive. It made me sad.

Many times, I would look out the window and wait for my father, who would never come to pick me up. I would whisper, "When will you pick me up, Father?" I really wanted to get back home as soon as possible.

I would walk alone to the babbling stream near the village. There were a small stone bridge there and many pebbles mixed with sand. I would gather the pebbles and build a replica of my house and its small gate. Then I would close my eyes and imagine my father coming to get me. He would kiss my forehead, put me on his back, and we would return to my house. I opened the imaginary door made of tiny pebbles and would spend some happy moments laughing by myself as I imagined entering my home and hearing the laughter of our family. There was a stone staircase in front of the gate of my house in Seoul. I could see myself jumping up those stairs, and in my dream the door to my house was right in front of me. Then I would awake with a start and open my eyes; it would already be dark, and the only sound would be the rushing water of the stream. I would stand up, surprised, and run home diligently, fearing that my aunt would be angry with me.

As a child, when I lived at my aunt's house, the men who worked at the house and the villagers would sometimes say and try to do sexual things to me. I had to defend myself as best I could. Even Mr. Yu, a teacher at the church's Sunday school took me to his house and tried to touch me in strange ways. I felt powerless in these situations. I was not strong, and I had no father to come to my rescue and stop them.

In that rural village, I was the little girl from Seoul with the pale face, the one whose bbal-gang-i, communist father escaped to North Korea with the rest of the family and left me behind. They always looked at me as something exotic. Eventually, I became like a porcupine, protecting myself from others.

At all costs, I avoided the barbershop, where a lot of men often gathered. They would say how pretty I was and try to get me to sit on their laps. I never went near them. Even if I experienced something that I sensed was strange or wrong, I had no one I could talk to about it. If I told my aunt, she would scold me and say that I was not being quiet enough. I was determined to be very careful and take care of myself.

When I went to my friends' houses, I would see their families gathered with one another, laughing, eating, and just enjoying themselves. For me, it seemed like I did not have an actual life as they did. I was living a fake life. When I saw them talking to their mothers, fathers, and brothers, being affectionate to one another, I would close my eyes and dream of my father picking me up. I hungered for the affection of my family, and I constantly imagined myself with them at my home.

When you lose your parents at an early age and become an orphan, it mentally exhausts you, and you live in a state of devastation. I did not have a family that loved me. I did not have an ordinary home life with a family that shared its love with me every day. Love was scarce in my life. When I heard these kinds of conversations at my friends' homes, I was envious, but I also found it unfamiliar.

I still often feel alone like this. I have lived my entire life with a strange sense of isolation and loneliness. Living in a home with those who did not want me at the age of four was bound to leave scars. No one understands how insecure I have always been about my life.

Even today, I am not always sure that I am doing a good job, even as the owner of my own company. I have always worked harder and harder for myself because I felt I had to endure everything alone.

As a young child, when I looked in the mirror and studied my face, I would see myself smiling brightly and cheerfully. At the same time, this face felt like a mask, covering up everything I was feeling.

What truly saved me during that time were the countless books I was always reading. Escaping into these books gave me space to dream. I would think about the future, about how there was always tomorrow. I tried to have faith that a better tomorrow would come, as it did for Little Orphan Annie who eventually found her way out of the orphanage and into a loving family. Even now, I try to push away all the negative thoughts before I go to bed.

When I was young and my aunt and her husband would go to her in-law's house for the ancestral memorial rites, or when she would go to celebrate Korean holidays, she would always leave me at home with the maid—I was always alone during every holiday.

I understood why my aunt did it. If I went with her, I would not be treated like family. No one was related to me. They were all tied together in blood or marriage—aunts, uncles, grandmothers, grandfathers, nephews, and nieces.

The same was true even for my aunt's family, the Park family. I would be with my aunt and my step-aunts, but I really had nothing to do with the Park family. My mother was only their stepsister. Her surname was Kang, not Park. Besides, my entire family was on the other side of the thirty-eighth parallel, and I knew nothing about their lives.

Members of the extended Kang family who were still in the South and lived near my aunt never talked to me either.

I grew up entirely isolated, with no family except for my aunt. I was glad to have her, even though I always felt alone and lonely.

Even when I divorced my husband, I tried to make sure my sons stayed close to their father and his family as much as possible. I made sure they visited his parents, prejudiced as they were, for all the American holidays until they passed away. My children spent every American holiday with their father and their grandparents.

During my life in Korea and in the United States, I have always been alone and felt very lonely during holidays. Despite my loneliness, I was happy my sons could spend holidays with their father, grandparents, uncles, aunts, and cousins.

***

In my homeland of Korea, people have identified themselves not only by surname, but by the geographical place where their family had originated. These origins can be traced back thousands of years.

The Koreans were a traditional tribal society with a clan structure. The society is intensely family oriented, and it places high value on genealogy and pedigree. For example, my surname name is Kim, but I can be traced back to the Kims that originated in the city of Gyeongju. I am a Gyeongju Kim. This name has a thousand years of history.

Kim Il-sung disrespectfully used this tradition to pretend that he and his family were of the Baekdu Mountain lineage. Baekdu Mountain is an active volcano on the North Korean and Chinese border. It is enormous and beautiful, with a significant importance to Korean culture. An old Korean creation myth places the birthplace of the Korean nation on this mountain five thousand years ago, through the transformation of a bear.

As the story goes, a long time ago, Hwanyung, the son of the lord of heaven ruled the humans. In Baekdu Mountain, there lived a tiger and a bear that wished to become human. Hwanyung gave them garlic and mugwort. He told them they could become human if they stayed out of the sunlight in this dark cave and ate only garlic and mugwort for one hundred days. The tiger gave up after twenty days, but the bear stayed and continued to eat the garlic and mugwort. The bear transformed into a beautiful woman. Hwanyung took her as his wife, and she gave birth to a son. They named him Dangun. He grew up to rule the Korean people and establish the kingdom of Gojoseon. It was the first kingdom in Korean history, and it started in Baekdu Mountain.

Kim Il-sung's regime manipulated this story to claim that he was a god and descendant of the Baekdu bloodline. What a bunch of nonsense! But now, their actions have made the Kim Il-sung bloodline more terrifying and vicious than any royal family name in Korean history.

For someone like me, an orphan, Korean society can be a cold, indifferent place. I had to survive in such a society obsessed with family ancestry—a little girl with a bbal-gang-i, communist father and family in North Korea. I grew up alone, a child of communists.

During the Joseon dynasty, the pedigree of people's genealogy was an essential element to their identity. The importance of family was at the center of the state. Westerners often looked upon the Joseon government as polite and courteous.

A North Korean extreme nationalism arose after World War II. This type of nationalism rejected all foreign powers regardless of consequence. There is even a North Korea–sponsored organization called Uriminzokkiri (which translates to "Between Our Nation of People") that exists to this day and promotes this dangerous type of nationalism. This organization even has some supporters among the Korean American community in the United States. Hitler's Nazism is an example of this type of nationalism in its worst form.

After the end of the Japanese occupation in 1945, this romanticized idea of nationalism gained popularity. There was a great independence activist named Kim Gu that promoted this ideal. He was a fierce antic-communist who worked hand in hand with Syngman Rhee to free Korea from foreign powers. Even though Kim Gu was at heart against the communists, he eventually was willing to work with Stalin because he falsely believed that Stalin would help unify the peninsula and then leave Korea to manage its own people. Unfortunately, this put him at odds with Syngman Rhee, who understood that Stalin's goal was to create a communist Korea. Therefore, Kim Gu did not acknowledge the formation of South Korea on August 15, 1948.

It was Stalin's dream to have a unified Korea under communist rule like what was happening in Eastern Europe. Kim Gu was taken by this communist dream—and for that he was killed by a young anti-communist named Lieutenant Ahn Doo-hee. His murder has been the subject of controversy and conspiracy theories that have lived on into the present day. Unlike some pro-communist supporters, I do not believe that Syngman Rhee or the CIA ordered the assassination of Kim Gu.

Dr. Syngman Rhee despised terrorists. He was a Christian and an idealist who believed in a true liberal democracy. I have read his book and believe that he and I share a love for democracy and religion. He was a patriot who dedicated his life to his country, much like Kim Gu. Despite their differences, I firmly believe that Dr. Rhee would not assassinate someone who truly believed in and worked hard for Korea's independence as much as he did.

Dr. Syngman Rhee truly understood the motivations of the great world powers. Even though he was staunchly anti-communist and anti-Soviet, he understood the complexity of the power struggle. He fiercely opposed the United States working with the Soviets in the occupation of the peninsula.

He fought hard to create the Republic of Korea and battled against any communist influence on Korea. He was a revolutionary hero of South Korea and a recognized world leader.

At the end of the World War II, Stalin's forces were powerful. Eastern Europe and parts of Eurasia had come under communist rule. Mao Zedong had swept China into civil war, winning it for the communists. The communists were taking root all over the world. Even in

America, Stalin had spies observing the US government. President Rhee had a keen understanding of the world.

With his hard work, Syngman Rhee gave birth to the Republic of Korea, which was officially recognized by the United Nations on December 12, 1948. This paved the way for a coalition of forces to fiercely defend the Republic of Korea when war broke out between North South Korea on June 25, 1950.

It was Stalin's aggression that made the thirty-eighth parallel necessary. Without the thirty-eighth parallel, Stalin would have pushed his forces all the way down to Busan, and Korea would be communist. Syngman Rhee spent his entire life defending and serving his country, yet he died in poverty and exile in Hawaii. In his final years, even the United States had turned its back on him. At ninety years of age, this revolutionary soldier died quietly and vanished into the pages of history. It hurts my heart to think of this great man's life coming to such a sad end. Someday, I will go to Hawaii and visit the final resting place of Syngman Rhee to pay my respects and express my gratitude for his work.

When Korea was freed from Japan at end of World War II, the nation had the naivety of a child. Korea certainly needed pragmatic leaders with the wisdom and understanding of global politics of the time. Instead, we had communist nationalists and romantic idealists like my father. Korea did not need the likes of Stalin and Mao Zedong. Korea did not need a repressive, communist, one-party system. Korea did not need leaders who took the lives of tens of millions of their own people. Korea did not need another oppressive state like Japan.

What Korea needed was the support of the United States and the United Nations, who wanted to help create a democratically elected government that respects individual freedom and self-governance.

I speak as a child of a communist. I believe that my father was a war criminal and a traitor to Korea. My father followed Stalin and Kim Il-sung who are responsible for a war that took the lives of 4.8 million people.

I wish I could talk to my father right now. I have things I want to say to him. Even though I have missed him endlessly all my life, I have also hated him for all the things he has done. My father's choices are the reason his life ended tragically. My family fell into misery because of him—but now I want to forgive him and love him.

Father, I forgive you. As a Christian, I forgive you. I know that God loves you and that you are with Him. I know you stood against the United States, but the United States military fought hard to win World War II and free the Korean people. The United States is a strong partner of many liberal democracies at the United Nations. This is why Stalin and the Soviet Union were wary of the United States.

My father, a member of the Communist Party of Korea and who supported Stalin and Kim Il-sung, was shot to death in North Korea in 1956. He was purged as part of a violent and bloody power move by Kim Il-sung. My family in North Korea was not even given his body for a proper burial.

I have lived in the United States for fifty years. I realize how powerful this country is, and I believe that the people and government have always been committed to making the United States a true democratic republic.

I myself am an American citizen who is striving for these democratic ideals. I believe that the United States is a place where a person can achieve their dreams if they work hard. My life is what it is today because I came to America and was given a chance. Even with all its shortcomings and all my struggles with racism and prejudice in the United States—I still believe in this country and this democratic ideal.

The experience of my lonely, troubled childhood made me work extra hard to improve my life in America, and now the loneliness and challenges have finally become a thing of the past.

***

My aunt was a very noble and intelligent woman. Her face was fair and beautiful. Her shiny black hair had a hint of hair oil and was neatly arranged in a middle part and bun. She had beautiful eyes, a softly curved nose, white teeth, and lovely lips. People were always taken aback by her elegance and beauty when they saw her white face and her always-clean jade hanbok. My aunt was a dignified first wife. As a little girl, when I saw her carrying her pretty parasol and wearing her jade hanbok, which rustled gently as she walked, I thought she looked beautiful.

A group of people in town put money into a rotating savings account called a *kye* in Korean. My aunt was the administrator of the account and protected and distributed the money. She was able to save a significant amount of money so that when her husband inevitably kicked out his mistresses for not giving birth to a son, she would be able to give them money to survive. She also gave part of her share to the town church where she was a deaconess.

My aunt was skilled at sewing and knitting. I went to school carrying a beautiful backpack that she had embroidered. Every winter, she knit me a pair of woolen pants and a sweater.

My aunt's radiant visage and generous spirit were known everywhere. At her church, the Sunday school teachers and pastors loved her. When she would come to my school to speak to my teacher, everyone would stare at her admiringly from afar.

Some of my meaner classmates spread rumors that I had become head of the class because of my aunt's reputation and influence. This made me angry because I knew how hard I had studied. I had also won first place in the church storytelling contest—at multiple churches, in fact.

My aunt was always very strict with me. She prohibited me from eating food while out on the street. Sometimes, I would steal American candy from the house and swap it with a classmate at lunch for sweet potatoes. Once I traded for a salted prawn so I could eat it out on the street.

The country kids would put their aluminum lunch boxes in a long white cloth and tie it around their waist. It would rattle loudly whenever they walked or ran. Because I liked that sound, I swapped my embroidered backpack for a lunch box. My aunt got angry when she found out, shouting at me and slapping me.

When I reflect on it now, my aunt was trying to get the best education for me. While some may assume that she was a naive country woman, she was wiser than any educated person from the city. Her life was very difficult. And even though we had our differences, we both shared a deep love for my mother in North Korea.

But sadly, my aunt never thought of me as her child—and she treated me that way. I have never felt like her daughter, and I never felt like her house was my home. I was just a temporary lodger at that house. It always felt like I would stay there for only a short while.

My aunt was very wise, but she could be quite cold. Because she never had sons of her own, she turned to the sons of others and played the part of a benevolent mother and grandmother. Later in the United States, she showed an exceptional amount of affection toward my sons. She also treated the priests at the Korean Catholic church in the United States as if they were her own sons.

One day, when my aunt and her husband got into a big fight because of one of his concubines, my aunt packed our things and we left the house. We moved to the city of Daejeon to live near her sister, my second aunt, who was already living there.

My second aunt had moved there to be near her cousin. She lived next to a small hospital that her cousin's husband owned. My aunt and I rented a small home near the hospital. I was in third grade and transferred into Samsung primary school in Daejeon. I was beginning a new life once again.

Her cousin's husband, Doctor Lee, was an obstetrician and gynecologist. My aunt's cousin lived very well as a doctor's wife, but she was very coldhearted toward me. Her daughters were students at Daejeon Women's High School. One daughter acted as if I did not exist, but the other treated me kindly. Her name was Joo-ja; she was beautiful and soft spoken.

Joo-ja would sometimes take me to the movies. We would see films like *Mogambo*, with movie stars Eva Gardner and Grace Kelly, or

Gone with the Wind, with Vivian Leigh. I was fascinated by these films. The thing that made me the happiest was the selection of books on Joo-ja's bookshelf. For me, these were the most precious treasures in her room—better than any goldmine. Through them, I met Sara the Little Princess, Little Orphan Annie, and the March Sisters. They were all right there in Joo-ja's room. Joo-ja was surprised that a little girl like me loved books that much, but she thought it was nice and said I could borrow as many books as I wanted.

One day, my aunt was at her cousin's husband's hospital, where she learned that she had at one time received gonorrhea from her husband, and it had gone untreated. Even though she had wanted so badly to have a baby, she physically could not have one.

When I went to visit her in the hospital room, where she was recovering from uterine surgery, I saw and ate a tangerine for the first time in my life. I put a piece of the fruit in my mouth, and it was like something you experience only in your dreams. The fresh, sweet juiciness in my mouth was an unforgettable sensation. I still think of this moment whenever I eat tangerines or oranges—that fragrant smell when I entered the room, my crying aunt as she ate this beautiful tangerine.

After the surgery, my aunt and I would often visit her cousin's home. My aunt also started getting occasional work making hanboks for money.

We used to visit an old friend of my aunt in Daejeon, and she would collect hanbok orders from friends and give them to my aunt to make. One day, she told my aunt that there was a decent man in town who had become a widower. She thought that my aunt was interested in finding a new husband, so she asked if she would be willing to get divorced and remarried to this man.

But my presence was a stumbling block to this plan. My aunt would have to leave me behind with my second aunt. I was sitting right there, yet they discussed me like I was a package or a piece of furniture. As they spoke, I felt very miserable. I was afraid that my aunt would remarry and leave me with my second aunt.

I still held hope that my father would come to get me. However, I was concerned and worried that he would not be able to find me when we moved to Daejeon.

That evening, my aunt made braised saury with daikon radishes. Usually, I enjoyed fish dishes like this even more than meat, but that day I could not stand the smell of the saury. It was sickening to me. My aunt looked at me strangely and complained. "Why aren't you eating? I thought you liked saury!" My aunt never could imagine the emotional pain I was often feeling, like an uneasy pit in my stomach. Even now, I do not like saury stew.

One day, six months later, my aunt's husband showed up unexpectedly with a bundle of red bean rice cakes, which were my favorites. I was near the door and could hear my aunt was crying, and in a soft voice her husband was trying to comfort her, asking her to return home. That was the only time I was ever thrilled to see my aunt's husband. I believed this meant my aunt would not remarry and abandon me. That was when we ended our time in Daejeon and returned to the rural town of Puyo. However, even though my aunt had that difficult uterine surgery, she still was unable to have a baby. And before long, my aunt's husband was back to misbehaving and bringing concubines into the house in the hopes that they would provide him with a son.

During that time, I was very lonely and read many books, desperately trying to overcome my loneliness through my imagination. I was obsessed with books from an early age. As a child, my favorite book was Francis Hodgson Burnett's *A Little Princess.* I read this book again and again, imagining the world within. In my mind, the streets of London were filled with fancy carriages, and India had mountains full of diamonds. Exotic landscapes unfolded in front of me. The book had a special magic for me because the protagonist, Sara, also had no father; he died in the far-off land of India. Though I did not believe my father to be dead, I felt a kinship to Sara. She had come from wealth and had a father who loved her. Then she lost it all when her father died. I was also charmed by the character of Mr. Carrisford, Sara's father's dearest friend and business partner. He had returned from India a wealthy man and spent two years desperately searching for Sara so as to bestow her father's portion of his fortune on her as well as provide her a loving home. It made me think of how my father must be searching for me.

But the most important thing about this book is that Sara, the little princess herself, always dreamed of bright and beautiful things, even in the most difficult of situations. She never lost hope, and she always treated people with goodness. I would often sit for hours on a sunny section of the floor reading *A Little Princess*.

I would sometimes close my eyes and imagine my father miraculously coming to save me. I thought that he could somehow make his way to me from North Korea through the Soviet Union and just appear in South Korea to pick me up. It is heartbreaking to think about it now.

When I would dream like that, all the terrible real challenges of my life would disappear into a magical mist. I think that reading many books as a child truly helped sustain me during that difficult period of my life—and I think God was also protecting me.

In the rural town where my aunt lived, there was a woman named Mrs. Min in a similar situation as my aunt. Because of her husband's concubine, she was living unhappily away from her husband with her young son and daughter. She and my aunt were very close friends, going to church together and meeting frequently. I would sometimes go to her house to see her beautiful flower garden. I found the scent of those flowers intoxicating.

Mrs Min's son, JK was in my class, and her daughter, SK was younger than me. SK was pretty and sweet, but she was very withdrawn and shy. The mother took care of her children very well and focused all her attention on them. I could even see signs of her love in the lunches she packed. She had raised her children even more attentively than the flowers in her garden.

Korean mothers are very protective of their children and often see other children as competitors to their own. They make great sacrifices to make sure their children are taken care of and succeed.

JK was in my class up until third grade. We both studied hard and did well. We both learned a lot at school, but I was always the head of the class.

My aunt frequently met with their mom and spoke with her as she would a sister. She would sympathize with my aunt because I was not really my aunt's daughter. She thought of me as a big headache for my aunt. This is actually how most people thought of my aunt's situation with me when I was a child.

In my heart, this lonely, desolate wind was always blowing through everything in my life. These children's father often visited them and gave them gifts. Despite his problems with their mother and his concubine, he loved his children. I would envy them very much for having a father in their life. And when I was alone, I would dream of my father bringing me presents, more presents than their father. I would look forward to this moment in my dreams.

Later, when the kids were old enough to go to high school, they moved to Seoul and graduated from one of the best high schools there. After high school, SK graduated from Ewha Women's University with a degree in pharmacology. JK graduated from Seoul National University and became a bank manager.

I was very envious of them, especially because they had a mother who loved them unconditionally and sacrificed for them. I slowly realized that expecting my father to return was not realistic, and the waiting began to turn into hatred.

***

For the last thirteen years of her life, my aunt suffered from Alzheimer's disease. For those thirteen years, I would visit my aunt in the dementia unit at a Minneapolis care facility every week. I was very impressed with the systems in place for dementia patients in the United States.

The United States has a solid welfare system to care for their elderly. In the US, many elderly Koreans do not live with their children—my aunt was no different. I divorced my husband at the age of thirty-five, worked thirty hours a week, and went to college full time while caring for two children alone. My aunt lived in a senior living apartment that had a Korean elderly care center. For most of her time in the US, she did not live with me or help with childcare. Instead, I had to help my aunt, who spoke very little English.

But she was still generous to my sons, saving up money to give them gifts. I am grateful for this. I am happy that my sons grew up loving their grandmother.

It was sad to see patients that did not receive visits from their children. For the ones that had a good relationship with their children, family members often visited weekly. Husbands and wives of patients came even more frequently. It did not matter whether the patient was rich or poor; they were all treated equally by staff.

A patient in my aunt's unit had held an important federal cabinet position when he was young. The family was wealthy and famous, and he stayed in the same kind of room as everyone else and received the same service.

Whenever I visited the facility, I would bring Korean treats and candy. The staff was always appreciative and took good care of my aunt. I was very grateful for them. It is not an easy job for those nurses and orderlies to deal with all the messiness and chaos. I would see patients yelling at visitors and staff, sometimes grabbing them. Some patients wandered around repeating themselves like broken records, telling the same nonsense story over and over. One woman would sit patiently at the entrance holding a small bag, seemingly waiting for someone to come get her, blankly staring at everyone. They were like characters in a strange, sad comedy, repeating their behavior continuously every day and night. It was sad to watch them.

Yet the staff there cared for my aunt and the others twenty-four hours a day. If she had even the smallest mishap or health issue, like a cut or a bad fall, I immediately received a phone call. Much of the nursing staff was composed of African immigrants—such a wonderful, caring group of people.

Watching someone with Alzheimer's is like watching someone slowly drowning in a swamp that leads to oblivion. Toward the end of her life, my aunt would forget to swallow her food. The staff would feed her and make sure she kept the food in her mouth. They would give her puréed food, and if it leaked out of her mouth, an orderly would have to catch it and spoon it back into her mouth.

Every time I visited her, I would have to reintroduce myself. My aunt did not know me at all. When I arrived, she would look at me suspiciously, wondering why a stranger was there to see her.

Some of the gossipy grandmas from my aunt's church thought I was not visiting her at all. They knew I was not born her daughter, and they thought I was failing in my duties. They may have been resentful because I moved her away from the facility nearer the Korean Catholic church they all attended. However, that place was not secure enough for her, so to do what was best for her, I moved her to another facility. Thirteen years later, she passed away in that facility.

Whenever I visited my aunt, I would always read the Bible to her and sometimes sing hymns. Her religion had been very important to her. I prayed with her every time I came. Based on some advice I received from a friend who works in the field, I would visit often, but I would not stay for a long time when I was there. Sometimes, my sons would join me, and for that I was grateful.

The relationship between my sons and my aunt was always very good. She was a sweet grandmother to my sons. She gave them a lot of love and lots of gifts with what little money she had. Because she wanted to keep her independence, she lived with us for only a very short while, but she visited often, and my sons have many good memories with her. When they visited her with me, it was because they truly loved and had a good relationship her, better than mine with her. I took care of my aunt more out of obligation than out of love. I did not have very much love for her because of the many wounds I received from her as a child.

My aunt was in that facility for thirteen years and received the excellent care until her death. I was especially impressed with the staff during mealtimes. They treated the residents respectfully, as elders, as if they were their own parents. They exhibited lots of patience even when my aunt would forget to swallow her food. I watched them care for my aunt for many years and was impressed by the level of care she got in the United States.

When she was ninety-five years old and nearing death, a hospice nurse sat in the dementia ward and took care of her. They all touched my heart with their service and care. They supported our family and her, even in her final days.

In the time just before my aunt's death, my sons and I went to visit her more frequently. One day, I was there with my sons, and my aunt, who had been sleeping, suddenly opened her eyes. I quickly ran to one of the nurses and told him that she had woken up. He rushed over, and gently put his hand to her face and closed her eyes. He explained that she had passed away.

My sons shed more tears at the nurse's words than I did. My sons called my aunt *hal-mo-ni,* which means "grandmother," and they loved her more than I ever could.

The nurse asked me if I could wait a little bit before contacting the funeral home so that the staff could also take some time and say their farewells to my aunt. Once again, I was most grateful to them for their kindness and for how well they had cared for her. Tearfully, I said yes to the nurse's request.

I then contacted my aunt's Korean Catholic church, seeking someone who could perform last rites. I was worried about contacting them because it had been many years since she had been able to attend mass there. With the help of some friends, I was able to get in touch. Both the pastor at my Methodist church and the Korean Catholic priest came to anoint my aunt's forehead and offer up prayers for her.

Additionally, many members of the Korean Catholic church came to my house, lit incense in front of photographs of my aunt, and bowed as we do to honor our ancestors. I was in tears when I saw so many men, so many sons bowing in honor of my aunt. I thought about all that my aunt had suffered by not having a son. My aunt had to endure all her husband's other women because she never bore a son. Eventually, they divorced, and she had to leave her husband's house for good. She was always lonely because she had no children—no son.

Three days later, we had the visitation. She looked peaceful and beautiful surrounded by floral wreaths in a coffin covered with red roses. My sons brought photos of her with our family and displayed them for all the mourners and guests to see. Many people gathered at the funeral home to pay their final respects. We had a short Korean Catholic service that evening.

The next morning was a perfect spring day in May with the sun shining brightly in a beautiful blue sky. We solemnly celebrated my aunt's life with a funeral mass at the Korean Catholic church. My two sons, my children's father, and the Catholic Liturgical President served as pallbearers.

I rode in the first car behind the hearse with my youngest son and my three grandchildren in the procession to the cemetery. Then we lowered my aunt into her final resting place after a small ceremony. Then, one by one, in that sunbathed cemetery on that warm spring day, we each quietly dropped a rose onto the coffin and said our final goodbyes.

My sons felt more sadness than I did. My youngest son Paul had expressed concern about his grandmother's headstone memorial, and we chose a design together.

At the funeral luncheon, my fourteen-year-old grandson, without anyone asking him to, went to each table of guests, bowed politely, and thanked them for coming. He did something similar at the visitation the day before. I was very proud of him. He was very mature for someone so young. Many of the guests were praising him. Even in this time of sorrow, I was proud of my grandson.

During the funeral, I was in tears thinking of my maternal grandmother dying during the war when I was only five years old. I thought of her shabby little coffin disappearing into the mountains. I thought about that sad and lonely little girl who lost her grandmother and could never return to her home—the little girl who lost her family during the war.

***

When Korea was still at war, many people saved their military uniforms or bought new ones and went to the market to have them dyed. The man who dyed clothes at the market would put the uniforms in a big pot of black liquid, which was fashionable to do back then. When I went to the market, I would stare at the pot of pitch-black water.

I was maybe four or five years old when the townspeople found out that my father was a communist. Whenever people called me a bbal-gang-i, a little red communist, I would look at my hands, seeing that my skin was not red. I would wonder, *Why do they call me that? I am not red. My hands are not red.*

Once I asked my aunt, "Why does father prefer red when everyone else uses black to dye their military uniforms? Now people look at me and call me a red child."

She was taken aback by this question. She grabbed me and scolded me. "Your father is not a simple laborer. He is not a dye-man working in the market. Your father is an educated man! He is a great man!"

Later, when I began to truly hate my father, I thought my aunt was wrong. I thought that a man should not be measured by his education or bloodline or profession. These are not essential traits—a man should be judged by how responsibly he cares for and nurtures his wife and his children as husband and a father. I thought my father was a terrible father.

My aunt lived a miserable, unhappy life—she badly wanted a child, but she could not have one. Her husband frequently brought home mistresses to live in the same house as my aunt. She fought with her husband often. Many of these fights centered around her husband complaining about my presence in their home. To protect me from these fights, she would send me away to my second aunt's house. Back then, my aunt kept a small second house in a nearby village for my second aunt and her daughters to live. This is where I would go when they were fighting.

On one very windy day, I heard the sound of furniture being smashed. My aunt and her husband were having a particularly violent fight. She yelled at me to flee to her sister's house.

I quickly ran out of the house as tears streamed down my face. I wiped them away with my hands and made the long walk to the mountain village where my second aunt lived. The wind was so strong that the tears on my face were dried up in the cold wind. I fought through the wind with all my strength. I walked and walked until I could finally see my second aunt's house in the mountain village.

I thought of my grandmother in my sadness. She had brought me here, but now she was in heaven. I wanted to say, "Grandma, I want to go to my home." I desperately wished to return to my home in Seoul. I often cried out loudly on that mountain road, walking alone. As I walked to that mountain village to my second aunt's house, I wept out loud, crying out, asking why my father had not come for me.

I thought of my house and the gate out front. I thought about my brothers fighting and playing with me and the neighborhood children.

A Little Girl's Dream
Hyon Kim

Once upon a time
there was a little girl

That little girl,
after leaving home
in the middle of the war
with her grandmother,
lost her way back home

Grandmother,
who took the little girl
out of her home,
left the little girl
and went to heaven

I want to go home,
said the little girl,
crying sadly
But Grandmother
let go of the little girl
and now she is gone,
so far away up to heaven

Little Girl Remembers
Hyon Kim

One day suddenly strangers arrived.
They put Grandma in a wooden coffin,
loaded it on to an oxcart,
and went to the mountain.

The little girl had seen
her grandma disappearing
into the mountain
and thought, Now who will take me
to her home?

Little Girl Sees

Hyon Kim

In the evening,
every house in the
neighborhood had lights on.

Under that warm light,
they are whispering,
even in the midst of war
whispering affectionately to
each other—their family
under the warm light.

The little girl
heard the voices of
Daddy and Mommy who
had left her behind.

With the children
whom she once fought with
her brothers

who always heard
the loud little girl.

One day,
the little girl knew
now that she was really alone.

Every night,
the little girl had dreams
of going home.

Even now,
she often dreams of
going home.

And she is going to
tell her dad everything.

She has to tell her daddy
all about strange too-touchy uncles
and weird church teacher.

The little girl
dreams of returning home
being carried on her dad's back.

The little girl's
face is full of bright smiles,
like blossoming flowers.

As I walked against that powerful, bitter wind to my second aunt's house, I knew no one was going to greet me warmly. My one cousin, annoyed by my presence, would always look at me and say, "Why are you so ugly?" She truly made me think I was ugly.

I would always anxiously wait for my aunt to come get me, and I gladly went back to her house when she did. The second aunt was unhappy that her son and her husband were gone because of the war, and the cousins treated me coldly. My cousins resented my aunt a lot. They were jealous of me. They did not think I deserved to be adopted by my aunt. They resented that she spent money to feed, clothe, and shelter me while they remained poor. I was only the daughter of her half sister after all. I was a Kang, not a Park like them.

On the way back to my uncle's house, she would always complain to me, "I cannot believe how rude they are! Your mother and father loved them and treated them like family!"

Many years later in the United States, my friends recommended I get therapy because of the childhood trauma I suffered. I recently went into counseling, but at this point in my life there was little for the psychotherapist to do. I have often wondered if it would have helped me earlier in life. My early life was not an ordinary one, and I know it had consequences in my later life. All those lonely years had a profound emotional impact. I felt much loneliness and sadness, but I thought I did not have the luxury of having mental problems. I continued to live the life of a porcupine, protecting myself and my children, working hard, studying hard.

Around the year 2000, I was very tired of my life. I was lonely, and life seemed difficult. I felt as if I had no one to turn to and my life was a failure. But now I am no longer lonely, and I feel much more satisfaction in my life. I live every day thanking God for even the smallest things. I feel faithful and protected.

I often wonder if I gained strength from the unconditional love I received from my father when I was very young. However, my hatred for my father was also a place of strength for me. My hatred for him often gave me the drive to deal with the hardships in my life.

***

It was my first year at the village elementary school, and we had just started learning Hangul, the written Korean language. One day, I snuck into my aunt's cabinet to look at the big hidden package of my family photos, my father's letter, and several books. I read the letter from my father, in which he told my aunt that he would come to pick me up in three months.

But I also noticed the novels—books by Tolstoy and others. I would secretly sneak them out to read. I felt like I was escaping reality and entering the world of the book. Sometimes, new books appeared in my aunt's cabinet too. I read them all, and problems seemed to disappear for a while. The books would feed my imagination and my dreams.

From then on, I was like a starving child that needed books to survive. I would read everything I could. If I was at a friend's house and found new books on their shelves, I felt like I had found treasure. I borrowed and read all the books I could get my hands on. I was hungry for books everywhere I went.

Even though life was hard, I remained optimistic and did not allow myself to grieve. I always worked very hard, no matter the task. When I was living at my aunt's home in the countryside, I would help with chores or run out to the rice fields or the vegetable garden to pick beans and green onions. I would cross the stream and wade through deep water to pick beans that grew near my aunt's rice paddies. My head was always full of daydreams and fantasies. I imagined I was a princess who was trapped there. Sometimes, as I walked through the fields, I imagined that a prince or my father would come rescue me. I would see snails in the rice paddies getting trapped in holes in the ground and command them like soldiers to go back to the palace. Often, I would get lost in my imagination, and it would get late before I returned to my aunt's house—she would scold me when this happened.

Amid all the sadness in my life, these were fun memories. There were so many books in the world. From very early in my childhood, I would read *Anne of Green Gables* and *Little Women* and open my imagination.

In my high school and, later, my military years, I would visit used bookstores in Seoul, Daejeon, Daegu, and Busan. I loved rummaging through these old bookstores. I was never interested in visiting teahouses, which were popular in Korean cities at the time. I loved book shops. I also enjoyed music-listening rooms where I would go to listen to Beethoven, Mozart, Chopin, and others. Even today, I enjoy classical music.

When I was in the sixth grade, my aunt sent me back to the city of Daejeon. She knew that if I finished sixth grade at my country school, her husband would never let me attend the junior high school in Puyo—and I would have to quit school. She sent me back to live with my second aunt so I could finish sixth grade in Daejeon and get into the junior high there. This was a wise move by my aunt because it prevented her husband from deciding my future.

I transferred to the same Daejeon primary school where I had previously attended third grade when my aunt had left her husband. Once I graduated, I was accepted into Daejeon Women's Junior High School, a very prestigious school in Daejeon. I had to pass a difficult entrance exam. I was happy when I was accepted and received congratulations from my primary school teacher. Nine of us passed, and we took photos with our teacher. I still have the photo taken in 1959.

On the day the test results were posted, I went to the school alone. The other students came with their families. When students saw that they had passed, the family celebrated with them. Parents embraced their daughters. Siblings congratulated their sisters. I pushed my way through the crowd and was delighted to find my name on the wall. I returned alone to my second aunt's home and celebrated quietly within my heart.

Daejeon Women's Junior High School had a lot of good teachers. Among them, I liked the English teachers the most. During English classes, I would recall the times I spent with Joo-ja watching Hollywood movies in the theater. I was excited to learn the language that I had heard in those movies. I started with the alphabet and quickly moved on to simple sentences. Every day, I memorized more and more English words. The students had a nickname for our English teacher—Tic-Tok. Every time he turned his head, a new English word we had never heard would pop out of his mouth.

I enjoyed school very much because I liked studying. It really was hard to stay at my second aunt's house. She still blamed my father for her son going missing during the war. Her husband went missing too. She presumed both were dead and had continued to grieve for them. Their absence was apparent in her life every day. She had to take work as a seamstress to earn money. And she became disturbed, talking to herself all the time and treating not only me but the entire world around her as a nuisance.

The younger of my cousins continued to work as a nurse at her aunt's husband's hospital. The older cousin brought home an industrial knitting machine and often worked in a dusty environment. She later suffered a long battle with lung disease and died before she was sixty. It was not easy for women to find good jobs in Korea after the war. It was a hard life for people like my second aunt and her daughters. Even with the truce, even with the end of the fighting, the war was a never-ending presence in our lives.

My life in Daejeon was a solitary one. After school, some classmates would gather and go to the stationery store or other small shops near the school. They would buy snacks and trinkets and have fun together. Because I did not have any money, I could not even dream of joining them. But it was also hard for me to go back to my second aunt's home. I was miserable and barely passed my first year at Daejeon Women's Junior High School.

I returned to my aunt's house and transferred to Puyo Women's Junior High School. I am sure my second aunt was not sorry to see me go.

Then, on April 19, 1960, a revolution broke out in South Korea. I heard from the newspapers and the radio that many students were participating in demonstrations against the Korean government. Syngman Rhee eventually resigned the presidency. The following year, on May 16, 1961, I heard on the radio that there had been a military coup d'état.

I suffered severe trials in my childhood because my father was communist. Whenever there was political upheaval in Korea, I would feel like I was reliving that trauma—so I tried to ignore the things that were happening in Korea.

Puyo Women's Junior High School is in the city of Puyo, about an hour's walk from my aunt's house. The city of Puyo is a historic place; it was one of the capitals of the ancient kingdom of Baekje of the historic Three Kingdoms that ruled Korea from 18 BC to 660 AD. It also has a history that reaches back to the Songguk-ri culture, which represents Korea's Bronze Age 2,500 years ago.

My aunt lived in a town in the countryside. The boys in the town went to school by bicycle, and the girls walked. We would walk to the ferry crossing at the bank of the Geum River that we called "Baengma-gang" or "White Horse River." Because the ferryman was never there waiting, we would all call out to him so he could come take us across the river. Once across the river, we walked to the Puyo Women's Junior High School. The school was just above the base of Buso Mountain.

When we walked home after school, we would pick wild burdock root and put it in our backpacks. My aunt used it to make miso soup with burdock. On some days, the boys on their bicycles would write love letters and drop them in front of their favorite schoolgirls as they walked, and then pedal off quickly. I would sometimes go to the bus stop and board the bus. The bus station was run by my aunt's husband's sister—a nasty, temperamental woman—and ride it to school. The bus would take us to the Gyuam-myeon neighborhood, and we would have to cross the river by foot on a narrow, shaky bridge. It was a very stressful, nerve-racking experience crossing that bridge. The bus would have to come across on a ferry with the other vehicles. When I visited Puyo years later, a new, modern bridge had been built, and I was amazed at how wide and large it was. I kind of missed that rickety bridge of my memory.

My time at Puyo Women's Junior High School is filled with good memories. I was a top-level student, excelling in my Korean writing and literature classes. My teacher even thought I might become a writer someday.

The Korean countryside is beautiful in the spring and the fall, and some of us from the school would hike to the top of Buso Mountain and sing songs at the Nakhwa-am, the rock of the falling flowers. Every spring and fall, we would walk to the Busosanseong Fortress at the summit of the mountain.

The Busosanseong Fortress is an important Korean historical site that was originally designed to protect Sabi, the capital city of the Baekje Kingdom. In 660 AD, it was the site of the last battle against invading forces and the fall of the Baekje era. A legend says that as the Silla and Tang dynasty troops closed in to capture the capital city and the last Baekje king, three thousand women jumped to their deaths from the top of the mountain into the river below in order to avoid being defiled by the invading soldiers. The place where they jumped from is known as Nakhwa-am, the rock of the falling flowers.

In the late spring of 1961, as I was in my third year of junior high school, my aunt's husband's secret sixth mistress gave birth. It was confirmed that it was the child of my aunt's husband and, most importantly, a son. One day, this mistress, my aunt's husband's newest concubine, proudly walked into the house with my aunt's husband in front of her, carrying her newborn baby boy.

This woman looked so ugly to me. She could not close her mouth properly because of her buck teeth, and her eyes looked like those of an angry bulldog. This concubine bragged in front of my aunt about giving birth to a son, who had not provided any children to her husband. She claimed that she was not a bar girl, but rather a widow.

My aunt's husband's sister, a matchmaker, was supposedly the one who found this woman for her brother, a woman whose job was to give birth a son for my aunt's husband. The matchmaker was also the nasty, inhumane woman who ran the bus station in the village. She would often bring a traditional shaman to the house to summon the spirits to give her brother a son. She hated that my aunt attended a Christian church. And she hated me because of my bbal-gang-i, father.

This is the woman that had sent those young nationalists to the house to kill me. She was also the one encouraging my aunt's husband, to take on concubines. With her strong support, the sixth concubine, the one with the son, demanded that my aunt, who was legally married to her husband, leave her own house.

Eventually, my aunt agreed to divorce him, which was rare in Korean society at that time. She had become exhausted with his behavior and ended her marriage to him. Then we moved out of her home in the small town in the countryside and took residence in the city of Puyo.

At the time, it was not unusual for women like my aunt, who had no children, to be beaten by their husbands, who would also take up mistresses. This happened despite a new law prohibiting adultery. On September 18, 1953, in the aftermath of the war, the Korean government passed a law declaring adultery illegal, seeking to prevent the exploitation of married woman by their husbands. It was a controversial act passed by a narrow majority in the Republic of Korea National Assembly, garnering fifty-seven votes in a 110-member assembly.

However, few people had heard of it—the women who had no children did not know there was a law that could protect them. Many women were forced to live with their husbands' mistresses because they could not give birth to a child, or more specifically, a son. In the end, their husbands often kicked them out of the house, just as my aunt's husband did.

The five previous concubines that had occupied my aunt's house were mostly bar girls—women that hung around the bar and entertained the men. I remembered one woman made delicious barley rice cakes. Another one was especially nice to me because she pitied me as a poor, wretched little girl.

The most memorable one to me was the first mistress. I remember her making strange groaning sounds every night in my aunt's husband's bedroom. I remember how loud she would laugh at the dinner table with her big gums. She was a barmaid.

This woman had a six-month-old baby, but my aunt's husband was not the father. During the early part of the war, he had evacuated Puyo and gone into hiding. He came back with this woman and her baby. The woman would sleep with my aunt's husband in a guest room while my aunt and I slept in the master bedroom. From then on, he would always have us stay in the master bedroom, perhaps in deference to my aunt's status as his wife. He would never come into that room at night, whether to avoid me or my aunt I am not sure.

Every night after the first mistress moved into the house, I would hear her making that strange moaning sound in the bedroom with my aunt's husband. I would also sometimes hear the baby crying.

Sometimes the crying was so loud and piercing, it seemed to make the entire house shake. One night, when the noise of the baby woke me up, I could see my aunt was silently weeping next to me.

But every morning, even after a night of the mistress moaning and the baby crying, my aunt helped the mistress prepare breakfast for him as if nothing had happened the night before. Then my aunt's husband would loudly eat his breakfast and go to work.

One day, this baby boy, who had been crying more and more every night, suddenly died in his sleep. That night, as if nothing had happened, the strange moaning continued, as did my aunt's quiet sobbing and sighing. My aunt fought with her husband every day, yet she continued to help his mistress prepare breakfast for him every morning, even after the mysterious death of her baby. And every morning, my aunt's husband would loudly eat this breakfast made by these two women, one his wife, one his concubine. He would occasionally glance at me while eating—looking as if he were a serpent and I were his prey.

Decades later, when we lived in the United States, my aunt told me the true story of the first mistress. One night, while she was sitting quietly in the bathroom, she heard a strange noise. She opened the door a crack to investigate and could see something happening in front of the kitchen water basin. She opened the door a little further and could see that the mistress was feeding lye to her baby boy until he vomited blood from his mouth.

She was most surprised and frightened by this sight that she quickly closed the bathroom door. Trembling like a quaking aspen tree, she quietly returned to her room and lay awake all night. The next morning, the mother simply said that her baby had died suddenly in the night. My aunt was shocked by this because she knew the truth. This was during the war, when all sorts of crazy, horrible things were happening. Because she did not think she could tell anyone, she just buried it deep inside her heart, bearing the burden of the truth alone.

Sometime later, my aunt's husband kicked the first mistress out of the house. My aunt's husband then brought home a woman with blood-red lips, who looked as if she had been eating mice. None of the other concubines made the strange moaning sounds at night—at least that was a relief.

Months later, the first mistress did return with a three-day-old infant. She handed the baby to my aunt and it said it belonged to her husband. Unfortunately, the baby was a girl, not a son. The mistress later brought her other baby daughter to my aunt, and my aunt took care of them both.

Sadly, one of the babies died. The doctor said the baby was very weak because the mother had gonorrhea when she was born. The baby was constantly sick and eventually died of pneumonia.

My aunt took great care of those children. She would take a small can of American condensed milk and mix it with boiling water to feed them. She bathed them every day. And while the one child died very young, her sister, Kwang-ja, grew into a healthy three-year-old girl.

My aunt would bathe me and Kwang-ja—even brushed our teeth every day with American toothpaste. However, one day, Kwang-ja's mother returned and took her child back. After that, I sometimes awoke at night to the sounds of my aunt sighing and crying.

The concubine with the red lips was not around for long. Others also came and went. I guess none of them were able to provide my uncle with a son.

Then one day, Kwang-ja's mother returned, and this time she left her daughter with my aunt for good. Kwang-ja was young, but she had been corrupted by her mother's lifestyle and she would sing the bawdy songs that she heard at the bar—songs not suitable for children. They were certainly not the kind of words that should be coming out of the mouth of a young child. After that, my aunt insisted on bringing me and Kwang-ja to church every week.

The fifth concubine was pregnant when she arrived at my aunt's house. Within seven months, she had given birth to a son. My aunt's husband was happy and insisted that the baby was his son. Now that he had a son, he promised my aunt that there would be no more mistresses brought home. The fifth concubine was eventually kicked out because he no longer wanted her—and she left without her son whom my aunt cared for in his mother's absence.

Over the years, my aunt had been setting money aside. Whenever these women were forced to move out of their house, she would secretly give them small sums of money and wished them well.

While we lived in that house, my aunt dotingly raised the son of the fifth concubine. Sometimes I felt like she loved him more because he was the son she could never bear. I heard her tell friends that she wished she could take him with us when we left.

After we left the house, the aunt's husband and sixth mistress declared that the boy was a son of another man. They abused him and beat him. The sixth mistress, who pushed my aunt out of that house and demanded they divorce, became the first wife of the household. She had one son and two daughters. After this, my aunt decided not only to leave her home, but to leave her hometown where she had lived all her life.

Before she left, my aunt organized all the blankets and clothes and did all the washing. She wanted to leave the house in order. Then she met with all her friends, especially her church friends. She had to make many arrangements, and finally one day she told me what day we were leaving the village.

That day, my aunt double-checked all the boy's clothes and belongings. Then she said goodbye, hugging the little boy and crying. We said goodbye to everyone, and with the help of teachers from the church, we pulled our small wagon of belongings and moved to the city of Puyo.

We moved into a rented space with one room and a kitchen. It was near a historic temple from the Baekje Kingdom era. The school I was attending had changed locations from its place near Buso Mountain to a place nearer to this small, rented room. My aunt lived with me in this new place until late fall, then she found the courage to move to Seoul. After life in the rural countryside, moving into the huge city of Seoul was a big change.

My aunt found a corner space in the Geumho section of Seoul that was right in the market. She opened a small alteration and tailoring shop where she specialized in making hanboks.

I could not leave Puyo until I graduated from middle school. Fortunately, the family of my good friend and classmate Jung-sook let me stay at her house. Jung-sook's father was a doctor and commissioner of Puyo County. They graciously welcomed me into their home, so I moved into their house with what little luggage I had. Even now, I am deeply grateful for their generosity.

Being in ninth grade, we always had to study when we came home from school. Jung-sook's mother doted on us constantly. They had a big storeroom with meat, fruit, and candy. I ended up eating a lot while I was at her house. After I graduated from junior high school, I moved to my aunt's place in Seoul. When my aunt saw me, she exclaimed, "How did you get so fat?" I laughed to myself thinking about all the delicious things we would eat while studying.

From a young age, my aunt had excellent tailoring skills. She could make men's and women's clothes. It was fortunate that she was very skillful. Now that she was in Seoul, she did not have to put up with all the concubines. However, she was still a woman without a husband, and very few options existed for women like my aunt. Usually, they had to find work in restaurants or teahouses or work as housekeepers. Had she not been extremely skillful at sewing, she would have to settle for one of these options.

My aunt's small shop had a Singer sewing machine, a small charcoal stove, and a small workstation next to the sewing machine. She sat in front of the sewing machine all day, pushing the pedal repeatedly and carefully pressing the hanboks with the small, long-handled, heart-shaped iron that had been heated in the stove. We slept in the little shop at night, in essentially the same place where she had worked all day. A small attic sat on top of the shop, and sometimes I would collapse up there just to get away from the store, if even it was a short distance.

My aunt was always tired. Listening to the whirring sound of the sewing machine all day and all night, I began to be disgusted by the sound. It sounded like my aunt's soul slowly being crushed under the weight of her feet as she pressed the pedals of the machine.

Soon my aunt began to have more customers. Among them were the neighborhood barmaids, teahouse girls, and hairstylists bringing in different kinds of fabric to make hanboks. Sometimes, a high-end Korean *geisha* would come to the shop with expensive materials in exquisite colors. My aunt would charge more for that work.

One day, my aunt broke down and cried. She resented her ex-husband. "He took all the money I had saved!" she said. "He is a very savage human being and a crook. I saved that money for such a long time, and he took it from me! He's a flea-eating human being!" I felt sad and cried with her.

But then she stopped crying and said to me, "I have only come to Seoul to send you to school here. I am working and making this money for you. If you can succeed, then I will have lived well." This was her promise to me.

I was grateful and happy. I was jumping with joy. I had taken the year off from school, and not being in high school, all I could do was attend church, cook, and read books in the small attic. It was one of my greatest pleasures to go to the used bookshop and find books I wanted to read.

In the spring of 1963, I tested into one of the best girls' high schools, Moo-Hak Senior High School. As always, I went by myself to see the test results. As always, I stood there alone, looking for my name on the list while the kids around me shared their joy with their parents, brothers, and sisters, who were crying, laughing, and screaming with happiness. It made me feel lonely. I thought about my father, whom I hated for never coming for me. Even now when I think about those days, my heart goes cold. My aunt had promised to let me go to that good girls' high school, and now I had gotten in.

I enrolled in school and was an eager first-year student, studying very hard. I would take a long walk over a hill to school every day. At school, the Seoul kids were very cold to me. A lot of them had come straight from the junior high school in Seoul and already knew each other, and often they would spend all their time together. They were always hanging out, buying donuts and other street foods as they went in and out of the stationery store in front of the school. They all seemed so carefree, fun-loving, and youthful, having fun at school with their friends. Sadly, I always had to study alone and think about the chores I needed to do for my aunt.

One day early that summer, my aunt suddenly decided to move out of the alterations shop and into a rented house. A pastor and his sons lived there. He was the pastor of the church in the countryside where we used to live. She told me that we were to take good care of them and the house and that when the sons went to school, we had to pack their lunches.

When we arrived at the house, the sons and I stared blankly at each other. One was in high school, and the other was in elementary school. The pastor, who was seated next to my aunt, smiled awkwardly at me. It made me feel uncomfortable.

I did not like the pastor. He was still married, yet let my aunt live with him and his sons. He was a pastor, but he still liked going to the teahouses where the young women went. He acted casually in a way that made me feel uneasy.

I began to wonder about the true relationship between Pastor Lee and my aunt. As the days went by, it seemed more and more inappropriate, which made me anxious. One day, I confronted my aunt about it. We argued, and I said something that I probably should not have. Trembling with anger, I shouted, "How can you live such a filthy life? You are no better than your husband's mistresses! And what about your promise? You said you came to Seoul so you could make money as a seamstress and send me to school!"

My aunt yelled back, "If it disgusts you that much, if you think I am so filthy, you do not need to stay in this house. You are not my daughter. You are just a little bbal-gang-i, communist bitch!"

As she was yelling at me, she threw my books, bags, and all my belongings out into the yard. She kicked me out of that house. It happened quite fast, like being struck by lightning. It felt most unfair. I left with only the items I could fit in my backpack. Now I was suddenly homeless.

I had been in Seoul for less than a year and had nowhere to go because I did not know anyone. After being kicked out of the house, I put on my school uniform, and with my backpack of belongings, I rode around on a public bus all day long. I sat on a bus seat and looked out the window, watching the streets of Seoul go by. I had very little money in my pocket. I got off the bus as the sun set and walked toward Namsan Mountain. Frustrated and sad, not knowing what to do, I climbed to the top of the mountain and looked down at the city below. The warm, flickering lights from the many houses of Seoul lit up in the distance. I had no place to go nor any family to greet me. There were just my tears and the sorrow in my heart.

I came down from the mountain and went to the nearest police station. I asked the officers if I could sleep in the station overnight. They were friendly, and some even invited me to stay at their homes. Instead, I just sat on a bench in the station. Because I could not sleep, I just waited for morning to arrive. I stayed only that one night at the police station, where I got very little sleep.

At the time, I was reading many books by many different authors—writers like Tolstoy, Dostoevsky, Nietzsche, Hermann Hesse, André Gide, Goethe, Thomas Mann, and Stendhal. Reading those books made me feel mature. I almost felt strangely proud, like an adult. Here I was—a schoolgirl, alone, sitting on a bench in a police station all night—and the next day I went to school.

I explained the situation to my teacher, how I had no parents, no home, and no family to stay with because my aunt had kicked me out. The teacher seemed overwhelmed and sent me to the school counselor, Mrs. Won. For some reason, she had me take an IQ test, which I scored very well on. Then she took me to a YWCA women's boarding house in the Huam-dong neighborhood of Seoul. Mrs. Won spoke to a large, scary-looking staff member before handing me over to her. Mrs. Won turned to me and said, "You can stay here for only a month. If your aunt comes to school looking for you, I will get in touch with you right away so she can take you back to her home."

I was grateful to Mrs. Won and felt fortunate that I had a place I could stay for the month. I graciously thanked her.

Once Mrs. Won had gone, the large, scary-looking woman, who turned out to be the house mother, brought me to my room. I shared the room with two women. Later, I found out that those women had volunteered to have me stay in their room after they heard about my situation. The house mother then took me back to the dining room, where many women were eating.

Later in my life, I would become a member of the national board of directors for YWCA USA. I felt honored to serve because I was still grateful to the YWCA for being there in my time of desperate need in Seoul many years ago.

That night, I slept in the boarding house, wondering what I would do in a month. I worried about it all night, not knowing what I was going to do with my life. I had nowhere else in the world to go. I was hateful and resentful toward my father. I had never hated him more than I did that night. I kept thinking about my father, who I had waited for, who I had longed for since I was four years old. He had never kept the promise he made in that letter to my aunt! He had abandoned me, his daughter, because of his communist ideology.

Strangely, I did not hate my mother and my brothers. I did not feel abandoned by them. That night I felt a desperation and depression deep down in the recesses of my heart.

I finally abandoned all my hopes of a miraculous reunion with my father. I abandoned my ridiculous idea that he might flee North Korea through the Soviet Union and make his way back to me.

After a few weeks passed, Mrs. Won told me that my aunt had not come looking for me. Almost every night, I was consumed with despair and anger. I was frightened because I was alone and I had nowhere to go.

***

It was 1963, but Korea still had not escaped the shadow of war. Nearly everyone struggled with poverty. There were not yet the many factories that would eventually be built and provide jobs for the Korean people. Decent job opportunities for women were especially scarce. Many became live-in housekeepers, barmaids, or prostitutes. So every night, I went crazy with worry about where I would go and how I would survive.

I would stay up very late worrying until I finally fell asleep. In the morning, I would wake up to the sound of my two roommates getting ready for work. The whole time I stayed there, these two women, Miss Park and Miss Shin, were especially generous and helpful.

Miss Shin was particularly warm and kind to me. She was a tall and sharp-looking woman. She would sometimes see me in the middle of the night, wandering about, mumbling to myself and crying. Sometimes, I would sneak out of the room and cry in the kitchen.

One night, Miss Shin quietly followed me into the kitchen and talked to me. We talked about our families and lives. She tried to help and give advice. We talked deep into the night, and we continued to have more discussions over the next few days.

Miss Shin had left her hometown of Gwangju and enlisted in the Korean Women's Army. She worked as an administrative female soldier. Then she got a job in Yongsan at a US army base after completing her Korean military service.

I saw how they dressed up nicely every morning when they left the house to go to work. Miss Shin was very sympathetic about my situation. One day she took my hand, looked me in the eyes, and suggested something that would become a significant turning point in my life: "I've been talking to you for a few days, and I think you can enlist as a South Korean female soldier with your skills. Training will be difficult, but I know you can do it. I will show you how to get to the

Republic of Korea (ROK) military headquarters. You can go to the women's army office to apply.

It was like a dream. I was very happy and listened intently to every detail as Miss Shin explained where to go and how to apply.

The ROK military began accepting woman during the Korean War on September 6, 1950. In July of 1955, a military training center for women was established in Seoul. In January of 1959, the training center was moved to the ROK army headquarters.

I was happy for the opportunity because it gave me a place to stay at the end of the month. I had spent many nights feeling desperate and hating my father. I just wanted to die—but hearing Miss Shin's advice gave me a hope—the tiniest ray of sunshine in a stormy sky.

The moment I opened my eyes the next day, I went to the women's military center at the ROK army headquarters and requested an application as instructed. Everything went very smoothly. I then went to my high school and spoke to Mrs. Won. With her help, I submitted all the paperwork and took the appropriate exam. I then joined the women's army.

It was 1963, and I was sixteen years old. I enlisted in the women's army even though I was still in my first year at Moo-Hak Girls High School. Until the early 1970s, women could join the women's military after junior high school. They accepted any qualified Korean women between the ages of sixteen and twenty-four.

It was a very different army for women back then. Opportunities for advancement were scarce; however, the Korean military has become more inclusive since then. Women were allowed into the Air Force Academy in 1997, the Military Academy in 1998, and the Naval Academy in 1999. In 2010, a Women's Military Education Corps was established at all of the major universities. Today, women can achieve higher ranks than they could when I was a member.

At the Women's Military Training Center in Seoul, the three months of basic military training were difficult and challenging. I had to undergo unimaginable physical training every day. Many women stopped menstruating during this time, and some even became incontinent from how hard they had to strain physically.

Some women gave up in the middle of this period and left the training camp. I was clenching my teeth, but I made it to the end. The mental strength I gained from enduring this extremely difficult training experience has been a huge asset in my life.

One day, we went to the military academy to practice shooting. During the shooting exercises, some of the trainees flinched at seeing a cartridge get ejected or hearing the loud gunfire, afraid they were going to be hit by a bullet; some even fainted.

But when I practiced shooting, I would say to myself, "Father, I am pointing this gun at you now," and imagined him in front of me. I found out decades later that Kim Il-sung had my father shot and killed in 1956—he was not even alive then.

Every evening, each of us would clean and polish our M1 rifles until they sparkled in the light. We would clean up our food containers and set our training clothes at our bedside. Once we passed inspection, we could sleep. We were all so exhausted that we could immediately fall asleep. Sometimes, an officer would blow a whistle that would scream in our ears in the middle of the night, and we would have to dress quickly in the dark and get onto the training ground. Once we were there, a sergeant would shout orders to us in her piercing voice, screaming at us as we were sweating and panting. We could always be called out for exercises like this. We were always on standby, night and day.

But despite of the many difficulties, I had a good life at the training center. It was a place to stay, and it gave me hope for my future life.

This was in the final months of 1963. I remember because I was at the training center when we received news of President John F. Kennedy's assassination on November 22. It was announced on the loudspeaker as we were on the training ground doing our exercises. We continued to train in silence.

After completing basic training, there was a test. Miss Shin had told me about this. Women were placed in certain training classes based on their score—telephone operator if it was low, Korean language typist if it was average, English language typist if it was high.

Because I scored well, I was assigned to take English language typing lessons. I stayed at the training camp for three more months learning how to type in English and perform administrative duties.

It was all as Miss Shin had described. I was grateful to her. I am also grateful for my religion and my faith in God for helping me get through this experience.

For three years, I was in the South Korean army. Three of my formative years, when I was first blooming like a delicate flower, I was a soldier, a brave soldier, who lived a strict and disciplined life. This time in my life remains a positive experience and provided me with a good education. In many ways, I am grateful to the Republic of Korea for raising me and helping me become an adult.

On the day we graduated from military training, they distributed a variety of necessities, such as stockings, women's military uniforms, hats, and black high-heeled shoes. This was the first time I had ever walked in high heels, and I loved the sound they made.

I was excited for the next phase of my life.

I became a private first class in the South Korean army. I had high spirits and lofty dreams. I regret that I did not take any photos at the time.

***

Today, I am seventy-four years old, and I am living very happily with my dog Suni, who is with me right now as I write this.

I am not lonely. Suni has been living with me for eleven years. Every day, she gives me unconditional love. She is also fiercely protective of me. There is something pure about the loyalty of animals; they are so different than humans.

Suni is a constant companion. Wherever I walk, she sticks to me like chewing gum. When I look at her, she looks back at me with child-like eyes. It reminds me of me when I was a little child. I was always waiting for my father or my aunt, blinking my little black eyes and staring off in the distance. Just as I waited for my father, longing for him to come for me, Suni waits for me every day until I come home.

I am not lonely. My sons come visit me in my home. I cook Korean food for them and my grandchildren. They enjoy all the Korean dishes I prepare. They also come see me on Korean holidays, and we celebrate together. They also know that Suni is very special to me and give her cuddles and love.

My friends also remark on how happy and well-loved Suni is. To me, she is the smartest and most loving dog in the world.

Suni, are you happy? I will come home every day and hug you and kiss you!

Entering prestigious Junior High School, 1959
(top row, 3rd from the right)
Credit: Photo Collection of Hyon Kim

CHAPTER THREE

I began my military career as a soldier at an army signal depot in Busan where more than a thousand soldiers were stationed. I arrived on a cold winter day in January of 1964. I remember feeling the biting wind. A crematorium sat on a ridge just above the base, a dingy gray smoke always billowing from its large chimney. It was during my time here that I began to advance in the military, and by the time I left Busan I had achieved my first promotion from private first class to sergeant. I performed typing and administrative duties at the base. I would work during the day, then go to night school at a girl's high school in another part of Busan. Every day, I would wake up early, perform my chores at the barracks, have breakfast, and walk to the base office to work. I would eat lunch back at the barracks and then work in the office all afternoon.

After work, I changed into a school uniform, grabbed my backpack, rushed out of the base past the gate to catch a bus. It took two buses to get to school, and then I would run a fair distance from the bus stop to get to the girls' high school. The school was near downtown Busan, quite a distance from the army base. Going to school like this every day made me feel like I was training for a marathon. I would arrive at school drenched in sweat. My face and back would be soaking wet, which sometimes would give me the chills.

I was in such a constant rush and had to study so much every day that I do not really have any fond memories of school. I cannot even recall having any friends. When I think back to that school, all the teachers and students are like faceless ghosts in my memory, shuffling back and forth to and from large, crowded classrooms. I do have a vague memory of a young girl who was a good singer with a husky voice; her voice reminds me of a famous Korean singer named Moon Ju-Ran who actually did attend school in Busan. I often wonder if it was her.

My favorite time was when school was over because I could stop running. After an exhausting day, I could stroll casually to the bus stop at night. I did not have to run breathlessly and worry about missing my bus. Many people were always waiting for the bus to the Seomyeon neighborhood near the army base.

At the bus stop, I could smell the delicious roasted chestnuts and sweet potatoes from the nearby street vendors. A bus girl would collect the fare, make sure we were all on the bus, then knock on the bus and shout "All right!" indicating to the driver that we could leave. The bus would then come to life like a giant beast and slowly move forward. I would stand inside the packed bus with my backpack, jostling about until we arrived in Seomyeon. Then I would change buses and head for the army base, returning to my barracks after an exhausting day.

I enjoyed listening to the southeastern dialect of the people in Gyeongsang province. It was fun to listen to them talking at the bus stop and on the bus. Because I was wearing a girl's high school uniform, people would not stare at me the way they would sometimes stare at female soldiers.

I spent a year and a half in the charming port city of Busan. On weekends, I would sometimes walk through the shopping district of Guangbok-dong or memorize the poems of Rainer Maria Rilke as I walk through the salty sea breeze.

Autumn Day

By Rainer Maria Rilke

Lord, it is time.

The summer was great.

Lay your shadows onto

the sundials

and let loose the winds

upon the fields.

Command the last fruits to

be full, give them yet two more

southern days,

urge them to perfection, and

chase the final sweetness into

the heavy wine.

Who now has no house,

builds no more.

Who is now alone,

will long remain So,

I will stay awake, read,

write long letters

and will wander restlessly

here and there in the avenues,

when the leaves drift.

On a base with more than a thousand soldiers, I was one of the only twenty-five women. We lived in a women's barracks in the same building as our superior, Captain Lee, who had a separate room. A long, large bedroom at the end of a hallway had twenty-four beds in two rows for the rest of us, as well as a bathroom with a toilet, a sink, and a small mess hall. We were together when we went to sleep—and also when we woke up in the morning.

It was similar to the basic training facilities but with fewer people. We kept the place spotless. To me, it was a great blessing to have a place to live, and I considered it my precious home.

During mealtimes, two soldiers were assigned to go to the main mess hall and retrieve the food for our squad. We would ride a small military truck to the headquarters building. At the main mess hall, a male soldier would scoop rice and soup with a shovel into giant vats. They would then load the food onto the truck, and we would drive it back to our barracks. The rice and the soup with meat and vegetables were delicious. There would also be kimchi and sometimes anchovies and gochujang (hot pepper paste). I have always been a good eater, and here was no exception. On weekends, most of the women soldiers went out into the city, which meant a lot of leftover rice. Often, I would dry the rice to save for a snack while I was studying.

Once I was an abandoned bbal-gang-i child of communist North Korea; now I had become a child of the Republic of Korea who cared for me until I was nineteen. I was grateful to have a place to rest, sleep at night, eat three meals, and study for high school. The 1960s were a difficult time for many people in Korea, many of whom lived in poverty. I lived my life with gratitude, thinking of my darkest hour when I had no home and nowhere to go. I studied hard, worked faithfully in the military, and lived my life as a joyful military woman.

In September of 1964, the first South Korea soldiers were dispatched to the Vietnam War. All of us participated in a dispatch ceremony at the military port in Busan. From that time on, we began sending letters of support to soldiers stationed in Vietnam. One South Korean marine wrote me a letter back and suggested that we meet when he returned to Korea. I was surprised and embarrassed by this. We never actually met because I had moved on to a base in Daegu, and he never sent me another letter.

The male soldiers were often protective of me. I was a seventeen-year-old private first class, but I was also a short-haired schoolgirl. Many of the soldiers said I reminded them of their little sisters, whom they had left behind at their homes. The guards at the gate would smile kindly and wave to me as I left for school in the evening wearing my school uniform.

On Sundays, I would go to the church on the base located right next to our barracks. I would worship with the other soldiers, male and female. Pastor Ahn, a captain, ran the church with his assistant, Corporal Lee, a young man with gentle eyes. Pastor Ahn had graduated from Yonsei Theological Seminary. He was a wonderful pastor who gave calm and intelligent sermons every Sunday.

Pastor Ahn was also fluent in English and served as an interpreter at joint military events with the United States. Sometimes he would even preach in English for the US Army soldiers. I had a deep respect for him. He was always very kind to me and even investigated getting me adopted by an American. Unfortunately, at seventeen years old, I was too old for adoption.

Sometimes, after the church service, I would accompany Pastor Ahn to visit some American missionaries. The living conditions for these missionaries were fantastic by Korean standards in 1964. It was at their home where I first saw a washing machine, as well as a stove and refrigerator in a heated kitchen. I thought it was an amazing, wonderful place.

On the way back, Pastor Ahn bought me my favorite snack—roasted sweet potatoes. When I would put the warm sweet potato in my pocket, it filled me with warmth. My hands, cold from the chilly breeze, would warm up when I placed them in my pocket.

In addition to visiting the missionaries' house, Pastor Ahn and I would go for long walks together and talk. As we climbed up a shallow ridge near the base, I told him about my parents and my sad childhood.

I told him about books I was reading. I told him about my dreams and hopes for the future. I also asked for his advice and opinion on everything, from university studies to English studies to life in general. I told him about my dream of going to college, and I said that I wanted to speak English as well as he did.

My salary was very small; the only clothing I had were my military and high school uniforms. I wore these two outfits everywhere I went. What little money I had went toward bus tickets, tuition, and schoolbooks.

Every weekend, the other women in the barracks would put on makeup, dress up beautifully, and have a fancy handbag on their shoulder as they left for the weekend. I felt as if I was living in a completely different world from them.

When the father of one of the women had passed away, she was given some leave. As she prepared to go home, she spent so much time crying—and then fixing her makeup—that it delayed her trip home. I found this to be an amusing set of priorities; I did not use makeup because I was a young student with little money. As an adult, I was more in the habit of wearing makeup and could not go out without at least wearing lipstick. I laugh when I realize I have become more like that woman.

I wanted to learn to speak English as well as Pastor Ahn. Occasionally, I would put on my soldier's uniform and go to the services at the US military base near where I lived. At church, I would open the English Bible and cross reference it against an English dictionary. I would concentrate hard on the sermons and try to understand what the pastor was saying.

I would also read American magazines I found there. I would look at the pictures of the blond, white students running around on perfectly manicured lawns. The American women who attended the service smelled like fragrant lilacs. The scent of their perfume often made me feel dizzy. The men dressed in nicely pressed suits. The women had beautiful one-piece dresses. Their children seemed so healthy. I was impressed by all of it, and I would sometimes dream of life in their country.

Today, I sit in my home with its well-kept lawn and stare out at the blue sky above the idyllic, peaceful lake shore and reflect on my past life. I have lived in the United States for fifty years and have overcome many adversities. I feel myself rooted in this land.

It was then, as a young soldier in Korea, that I got my first glimpses at a life in the United States. I knew it was the destination of my dreams—where I wanted to make my future.

It was my dream to move to the United States, a country that was built on the very freedom that my father abandoned because he chose communism. I wanted to live as a citizen of a free country, not a communist country. And I wanted to leave behind all the pain and suffering that I had experienced in Korea.

But at that time, my dream was in contrast with my reality, which was much darker. My two years of military service was coming to an end. Most people were excited about their discharge day—but I had not yet finished high school and had no place to go.

In the end, I decided to stake my future on the military. I reenlisted into military service as a sergeant. It made me unhappy, but I had no family and nowhere to go. It was the best choice I could make at the time.

I was given some leave and used it to take a train to Seoul. I visited the church where my aunt attended. I found out that soon after kicking me out of their home, my aunt had left the pastor. She had become frustrated with his immoral behavior and frequent visits to teahouses. She ended up getting remarried to the father of one of the church's lay ministers and was living with him. My aunt told me that she married him because she had no child to care for her. It made me sad to hear her say that.

Our relationship was always like that. She never truly accepted me as her child. There was always this cold wind consuming my heart. The loneliness sometimes drove me into unbearable sorrow.

Her new husband was originally from North Korea and was the son of a rich landowner. He had been a gentleman with a high education. After the liberation from Japan and the division of Korea, the North Korean government seized all private property, including his. He escaped and moved to Seoul, where he was practically penniless and lived in a little shack with my aunt in a depressed neighborhood. Because it had no room for me to stay there overnight, I left and went back to Busan with tears in my eyes. I missed that time when my aunt and I were together in the sewing shop in Geumho-dong Market.

I was seventeen, and it was my first vacation from the army. After that, I did not visit her again. I could not stand to see my beautiful aunt live in such poverty. From then on, when I had leave, I just stayed in the barracks and took day trips to different parts of Busan, like Haeundae beach, the fish market, or the markets on Gwangbokdong Street.

It was very sad. I had little money, no home to visit, and really no place to go on vacation. Someday, I would like to go back to Busan and walk along Gwangbokdong Street, see the Yeongdodaegyo Bridge, and visit Dongbaek Island off Haeundae beach. I want to go back and retrace the footsteps of that young girl in 1964 wearing a military uniform walking around Busan. I would like to peer into her heart and feel her loneliness as well as her hope and longing for the future.

One day, as I was working diligently at the army base in Busan, an old church teacher Mr. Yu came looking for me. He had sexually abused me when I was a little girl. He was now a captain in the ROK army and was on leave from the Vietnam War. When he came to the base to visit me, I refused to meet him. Nevertheless, he continued to show up at the base and ask to meet with me. He even showed his disgusting face at the office where I worked.

I kept refusing to meet with him, and he even talked to my superior, the captain from our barracks. She got angry with me. "Why won't you meet this man? He is a hero fighting in Vietnam for our nation!" She punished me by hitting me with a stick. Then she forced me to meet with him. The captain was a coldhearted woman. Other than this instance, I have no recollection of anything else about her, not even her name.

I had no choice but to dress up in my military uniform, put on my hat, and go out with him in Busan. We watched a movie together, and I had dinner with him. It was getting late, and I was worried about getting back to the base. He volunteered to take me back by taxi. I was relieved because it seemed like the day was going to finish without incident.

But in the cab, he suddenly changed his mind and asked me to stay with him overnight. He ordered the taxi driver to turn the taxi toward the Haeundae beach resort. I was shocked, I raised my hands, weeping, and pleading to the older taxi driver to take me back to the base. I told him if he has a daughter at home to save me for her sake. The driver turned the cab around and headed toward the base. It was a miracle. I told Captain Yu to get out of the taxi. The driver stopped the cab and Captain Yu, looking embarrassed, got out of the car.

Perhaps the driver took pity on me because he could still see the short-haired little schoolgirl behind the woman in the military outfit. I looked at this old man driving the taxi and was grateful for his kindness. I was accustomed to taking the bus. I knew that I did not have enough money in my pocket to pay him. I asked him to wait for me when we got to the base, and I ran to the barracks and got money to pay him. I was grateful to him for taking pity on me and preventing a terrible situation.

***

Early in the summer of 1965, I got promoted to sergeant and left Busan for a military base in Daegu. When I arrived, I was surprised by the enormous size of the base and the large number of women soldiers stationed there. It was a very serious place with well-trained, well-disciplined soldiers.

The base had many female senior officers, and the preferred instrument of discipline for those officers was beatings with a stick.

Everything was different from the smaller Busan signal depot. I knew that I did not want to stay there. I wanted to graduate from high school, get a job, and get discharged from military service as soon as possible.

The students at the girls' night school in Daegu were very friendly and down to earth. They called each other crude names and would joke and laugh. They were much more approachable than the students in Busan, and I felt more affectionate toward them.

In Daegu, I took an army bus daily from the women's barracks to my job at the ROK military office. During my commute, the bus would pass by the United States military base nearby. I would always think of Miss Shin and her advice every time I passed by there. I vowed to get a job at the US base just as Miss Shin did.

Every day, while I worked for my superiors in the office, I also worked toward this goal. Whenever I had time, I would diligently study English and practice typing on an English typewriter that I had stashed in a janitor's closet. As a result of that effort, I passed the English conversation test and the English typing test at the US army base. I also passed the US military civilian office exam without anyone else's help—but none of this helped with my most serious problem.

Although I qualified for new job with the US military, I was still a South Korean soldier. I would have to continue to serve as a sergeant in the ROK army for the duration of my enlistment period.

Then I remembered my cousin, who was never very nice to me, had a brother-in-law working in the personnel division of the South Korean army in Daegu. My cousin married a professor and was always embarrassed about her family and relatives. On one occasion, my aunt and I visited her, but she kicked us out of her house. After that, my aunt never saw her again. My situation was too urgent to let past grudges stand in the way. I dressed up in my military uniform and took the train to her house. To my great relief, her husband, a good-hearted man, welcomed me into their home. I could understand what my cousin saw in him and was grateful that he was willing to help.

My cousin's husband introduced me to his brother-in-law, an ROK colonel. The colonel smiled and said, "Sergeant Kim, I have heard you want to leave the army. So, do you have a lover?"

I was embarrassed and nervous. My heart trembled. "No, sir! There is no one like that."

Then he continued to smile and said, "No? Well, that is a problem. If you want to leave the military, there is only one way to get out. You must get married! Talk to your cousin again. Perhaps her husband might help you find a groom. Come back when you have solved this problem."

I talked to my cousin and her husband. He had one of his students sign a paper that said we were engaged to be married. This was how I able to leave the military. I expressed my eternal gratitude to my cousin and her husband. Once again, when I was in crisis, fate intervened and provided a solution. I thank God for the courage He gave me to persevere during these times.

I then received a letter from the US military personnel division in Daegu. The military police department on the US base in Waegwan, which is near Daegu, was looking for a woman to be an administrative assistant and a guard. The unit that hired me was a K9 unit where the guards were mostly men. My military experience and my administrative skills made me ideal for the job. I was pleased that they hired me for the position.

I worked as a secretary admin to the provost marshal during the day and as a security guard for the military police in the evening. Every day, I would go to my administrative job at the MP office at 8:00 a.m. Then I would go to the main gate and work as a security guard at four in the afternoon and work until 7:00 p.m. The job had become available because the woman who previously worked there got married and immigrated to the United States.

I was happy. It felt like a miracle.

Overcoming these crises have strengthened my faith in God. I feel like I was provided with the tools I needed at just the right time. I became homeless as a teenager, but then I was led to joining the military. The rigorous training and experience I received there provided me with tools that I have used throughout my life. Then, when I needed work, at a time when jobs were nearly impossible to get, this US military job, which perfectly fit my qualifications, became available.

Because the position involved training and working with a guard dog, the salaries for guards in the K9 unit were higher than most. Only two female guards were in this position. In addition, most of the security guards were subcontractors, only the K9 unit was run by the US army. It was unusual to be able to get a job like this directly with the United States military. I was very fortunate to be able to acquire this rare, high-quality job without any bribe money or special connections.

The US military gave out bonuses twice a year on Christmas Day and Independence Day in July. My salary was three times what a teacher at the Waegwan High School made. It was a considerable amount for a nineteen-year-old woman, and it was a dramatic change in my life.

After many twists and turns in my life, I was able to leave the Korean military and get a job in the US military. I immediately found a lodging house in the city of Waegwan run by the mother of a man who would become my lifelong friend, Professor Moon.

I then wrote a letter to my aunt, who was still struggling in Seoul. I asked her if she wanted to leave behind her life in Seoul and come live with me. I told her I would take care of her. She was still living with her second husband in a poor section of Seoul with no prospects. She quickly abandoned her life in Seoul to come live with me. She also converted to Catholicism. She said she wanted to follow the religion of my mother and grandmother, who had converted during the Korean War. I think perhaps there was an additional reason. One time, her second husband's daughter came to the Methodist church in Waegwan looking for her. Converting to Catholicism may have helped her stay hidden from her second husband, whom she had abandoned.

I also converted to Catholicism to be with my aunt. We formally enrolled in the Waegwan Catholic Church, and after six months of study we were confirmed in the church. I had been baptized Catholic and given the name Maria when my family converted in 1950. I kept the name Maria. My aunt was baptized with the name Rosa at the Waegwan Catholic Church. My aunt attended the Catholic services for the rest of her life until Alzheimer's disease restricted her to the dementia ward in 1998.

The next year, I went with my aunt to Puyo to retrieve my grandmother's remains from her grave to bring to the Catholic cemetery in Waegwan. In Korea, it is very important to be able to visit the graves of your ancestors and honor them on certain holidays. Because my aunt did not want to see anyone she knew in Puyo, I asked my grandmother's nephew to help me with this task. On a country road, we hiked up to the side of the mountain and found my grandmother's grave. I thought of my grandmother, buried in that mountain, all alone in the middle of the war. I was so heartbroken that I could not say anything. I simply cried softly.

It had been long since my grandmother and I had traveled to Puyo. She went through hell during the Korean War. Then she left me behind and went to heaven. Toward the end, she could not close her eyes but kept calling my name until the last moment of her life. As I approached her grave, I sobbed as I thought of her, my grandma.

But that seemed long ago. Now I had grown up and made my own money. I could move her remains to Waegwan—and that made me happy.

When my aunt moved to Waegwan, I moved out of the lodging home and rented a big house for the two of us. My aunt was amazed at how much money I made. I gave my salary to her and let her manage the household finances. We had a big house, and she rented out a few rooms to other families. She also served diligently for the Waegwan Catholic Church. She would often travel and help members living in more remote areas in the countryside. At the time, Korea had no funeral homes, so my aunt helped church members prepare bodies for funerals and burials. She was also a very good midwife.

We lived a good life, the two of us. My aunt seemed rejuvenated. The nobility and beauty returned to her face. I was making good money at the US army base. My aunt was very active in the church and was making friends. She was happy with our neighborhood. Our five years in Waegwan were happy times.

In the lodging house where I lived my aunt came to the Waegwan, I met Professor Moon, the son of the woman who ran the house. At the time, he was not a professor, but that is how I address him now. At the time, he was a first-year high school student in the nearby city of Gimcheon. He was fresh-faced and young, three years younger than I was, but he was mature in his manners and well behaved. The first time I met him was when he came home for spring break. He had a calm, adult-like demeanor when he conversed with his mother and sister. His mother was an excellent cook, and I was delighted to have such a perfect place to live.

Professor Moon and I exchanged letters and built a friendship over the next three years as he attended high school. I would share with him the writers and books that I had loved—the Greek classics, Goethe, Tolstoy, Dostoyevsky, Stendhal, André Gide, Hermann Hesse, Thomas Mann, Kafka, Nietzsche, and many classic American writers too. I also talked about Beethoven, Mozart, and Chopin, which I enjoyed listening to in the classical music rooms in the city.

We exchanged letters for three years, and through a shared love of books and music, we started to build a friendship. We shared knowledge, encouraged each other, and discussed our dreams for the future. Many years later, he told me those letters had a profound effect on his life. I was touched when he revealed that he had kept those letters all those decades later.

After graduating from high school, he attended Kyungpook National University in Daegu. On vacations and weekends, he often came to our home to visit my aunt and me. My aunt, lacking a son of her own, always adored him and treated him like a son.

In those days, we spent much of our time encouraging each other's dreams and hopes as we hiked through the acacia forests, rice paddies, and bean fields. He would always stop by our house before returning to his home to eat my aunt's delicious ramen with eggs and green onions. Even when I was not at home, he would come and spend time with my aunt and eat ramen before returning to his house. He told me that even today he can still remember the taste of the ramen my aunt made for us.

Professor Moon eventually earned his PhD from Kyungpook University. He became a university professor, earned tenure, and is now retired.

When I decided to get married and move to the United States, Professor Moon sent me a ten-page letter outlining all the shortcomings of an international marriage, arguing that I should marry him instead.

Our friendship has gone through many twists and turns, but it remains constant like water from the deepest well. I am always touched by his steadfastness and consistent heart, which I have not experienced much at all in the United States. Through him, I feel close to the spirit of my homeland, my Korean-ness. Sometimes we have gone years, almost decades without seeing one another, yet our friendship remains. Unlike my brothers in North Korea, I am able to see him in person when I want.

Now he is a retired professor, proud husband, father, and grandfather. He lives a harmonious life in Korea. I feel as if my years of loneliness and the weight of my life in a distant country created pain that prevented me from returning the kindness shown to me by Professor Moon.

***

Waegwan was a unique town. On the outskirts of town was the US military base, and nearby was a Benedictine abbey, the largest and most famous Catholic monastery in Korea. Male monks dedicating themselves to living a godly life existed just outside of a large military facility and all the illicit activities that come with it. Two completely different worlds lived practically side by side.

Just outside the back gate of the army base were bars lined up on both sides of the street. Day and night, the steady beat of American music would pour out loudly from the bars into the streets. Korean women and US soldiers would hold hands and drunkenly stagger down the streets, dancing to the music.

On the base, I worked as an administrative assistant in the provost marshal's office. The provost marshal was the head of the military police on the base. In my capacity working with the military police, I saw a lot of reports of accidents and crimes on and near the base. There was an administrative position that was usually occupied by a private first class looking to advance to sergeant by the time they returned to the United States. A master sergeant was the general manager of the office. Then the Korean administrative clerk was my position. When I started to work at the US army base at the age of nineteen, everything seemed new and miraculous.

At first, my English was quite clumsy, and I would get easily confused. I worked with a white sergeant with a pointed, bladelike nose who was a terribly bossy man. He was very particular about phone etiquette and nagged at me to answer with "the provost marshal's office, Miss Kim speaking." I could never say it quite the way he wanted because the words would get jumbled in my mouth. It gave me nightmares.

Besides answering the phone, I had to make coffee for the office staff and guests. I also had to transcribe handwritten statements from US soldiers sent from the military police desk. It was difficult for me to read that messy handwriting and type it on the English typewriter. My favorite task was to type letters for the provost marshal on paper that had a fancy seal.

The criminal statements I had to transcribe often had a lot of slang and profanity. I learned almost every dirty word in American English. On one of my first days, I could not find a certain word in the English dictionary, so I asked one of the American clerks if they knew what this word meant. He asked me to spell it out loud, and I started to say,

"F – U – C . . ." Everyone started laughing—but I could not understand why.

Each day I worked at the provost marshal's office, I learned a little bit more and got better at my job. Occasionally, I was also sent to work at the Criminal Investigation Division office.

I had a good job, and I was earning a good living. Although I was very happy living with my aunt in this situation, I had a fear in the corner of my heart about how long this happiness would last. For the first time in my life, I felt a sense of security, and I did not want to lose that.

Life as an employee of the US military was dynamic and frantic, with many interesting things always happening.

In our office was a clean-cut corporal who worked as a clerk with me. He was the son of a bank executive in New York. Before he joined military, he was a student at Columbia University. One day, he was given a gift from his fellow soldiers for his birthday. As soon as he unwrapped it, his face turned red. The gift was a framed cartoon from *Playboy* magazine. It was a satirical cartoon showing a doctor stabbing a man's buttocks with a long, fat needle to treat a sexually transmitted disease. As it turned out, this clerk who I saw as a nice, clean-cut gentleman contracted STDs rather frequently. The gift was intended to make fun of him for this.

My first experiences at the base made me think all US soldiers were spoiled and uneducated, only reading vulgar magazines like *Playboy*. Later I knew this was wrong—that some had less-vulgar tastes. One thing almost every one of them did have in common was that they were counting down the days until they would be discharged from the military.

On one side of the office, a sergeant sat at the large front desk where he would handle all the issues of the many MP soldiers constantly rushing in and out of the building. Across the hall was a small jail cell. When I would come to work in a miniskirt, I could hear the whistling and screaming as I walked down the hallway past the jail.

When I told this to my aunt, she was shocked and retailored my skirts so they went past my knees.

As time passed, I gradually adapted to working at the army base and with the people there. I also learned a lot about the United States as a nation, which seemed so remote and distant. I learned about it from the young soldiers who would sometimes erupt with stories about their home in loud and excited voices.

I learned about the Vietnam War that had just begun in 1964, a year before I arrived at the base. I learned about the Gulf of Tonkin incident and how the war order was signed by President Lyndon Johnson. I learned that President Kennedy, who had been assassinated in November of 1963 while I was still a Korean soldier in training, had opposed war in Vietnam.

As the days went by, the US soldiers who had become my friends and colleagues on the base began to get reassigned to fight in the Vietnam War. One by one, their friendly faces disappeared from the base. However, instead of going back to the United States as they dreamed of doing, they went to Vietnam where everything was unfamiliar and the weather was hot. This continually happened during my time working at the base. Every time I heard the sad news that one of my friends had been killed in Vietnam, I wept with the other soldiers. I thought about how they would carry around high school graduation photos of pretty girls back home whom they had hoped to marry someday.

In the office building where I worked, the large room with the MP front desk was always a busy place. I worked in an adjoining room, which was the master sergeant's office. It was me, the master sergeant, and a US soldier working as a clerk. Adjacent to this office was the provost marshal's office.

Other Koreans worked in the building too. A huge office managed the pass cards for all employees on the base. They also dealt with VD cards and related paperwork. VD cards were part of an attempt by the US military to combat the spread of venereal diseases among soldiers—and also to regulate Korean sex workers. Korean women working as sex workers had to go weekly to the health center and get tested for sexually transmitted diseases. A Korean man named Mr. Suh worked as an interpreter and a clerk for this office.

In the office opposite the bathrooms (our building had men's and women's, which was a very rare thing in Korea at the time), there was a security guard's office where my boss, Mr. Choi, worked. He also had a secondary office near the military guard-dog-training area. Mr. Choi was very neat and well put together, but he was also very bullying, and his presence frightened me. Like my aunt's husband, he generally ignored me or was dismissive of me as if I were invisible and unimportant.

Mr. Choi once told me, "Every woman who has previously held your position married a US solider and quit her job. Therefore, we are always having to hire new people." He said it as if he assumed that I had plans to do the same—thus he would look at me with contempt. While obviously women were in the military at the time, South Korea as a society still looked down on the idea. Mr. Choi was no different. Plus, because I had come into this position without offering him any sort of bribe, of course he did not like me.

I would often see the K9 security guards going in and out of Mr. Choi's office during the day. Among them, a Korean woman usually stood guard at the back gate. She had a piercing glare that people found unsettling. She would never speak to me. She just smiled and looked me over with those piercing eyes. It turns out she was a wealthy woman who had owned five different houses during her long tenure as a security guard. The rumor was that she made extra money on the side. I never really knew her because she never invited me to her drinking parties.

Outside the back gate of the army base, a completely different world unfolded, separate from the base and from Waegwan. Bars lined the streets, and the music was roaring night and day. Among that were all sorts of shops and travel agencies that took US currency, as well as houses where US soldiers visited and sometimes lived with Korean women.

Many of these Korean women who lived just outside the army base would go in and out of the base through the back gate. Sometimes, they would gather at the door and ride together in an army truck to go to a military club on the base. To come through the gate, they were required to show their VD cards to a female guard named Miss Choi. She was strong and intimidating. Many of the woman were afraid of her. Sometimes, when Miss Choi was away, I stood guard at the back gate in her place.

As I would check the VD cards of the Korean women, I found myself questioning why it was only the Korean women and not the US soldiers who had to line up this way and declare they were free of venereal diseases. Of course, I kept this thought to myself because I wanted to keep my job—but I did wonder.

The South Korean employees on the base had all sorts of derogatory names for the back gate. They called it the "Western Whore Gate," "GI Bride Gate," or "Yankee's Gate." Many were reluctant to use the back gate and thus avoided it.

I lived with my aunt in a rented house close to the Catholic church near the main entrance of the base. We had a comfortable life in Waegwan and lived there for five years. On October 2, 1966, 128 Korean nurses boarded a plane at Gimpo Airport on their way to West Germany. These were the first of a large migration of Korean nurses that came to Germany as part of a formal guest worker program called Gasterbeiterprogramm.

These Korean nurses went to this foreign country and worked very hard doing difficult tasks and caring for patients. Overcoming language and cultural barriers, these women were recognized by many German hospitals as exceptional workers.

From 1965 to 1975, Korean nurses working in Germany earned over $100 million in foreign currency, much of which was sent back to Korea to help rebuild our homeland. They set a good example of the Korean work ethic amid difficult circumstances and are considered patriots.

I sometimes think of their lives and how similar they are to mine and others like mine. The Korean women that worked on US bases and married US soldiers also faced difficult circumstances. This included both people employed by the base and sex workers. Yet Korean society has rejected us for so long, discriminating against us, calling us "foreign whores" or "GI brides." Some actually even threw stones at us. I do want to say that we are all patriots, even the sex workers, just like the Korean nurses who went to Germany.

Working our jobs on the bases, we earned foreign money that was invested into the Korean economy. As part of the US military police, we protected and saved the wives and daughters of Korean farmers who had been previously humiliated and raped by foreign soldiers during the Korean War.

When we came to the United States, we continued to sacrifice for our families in Korea, sending money to them from the US. We helped family members come to the United States to study and even to immigrate.

We have helped many of our brothers and nephews to live successful lives here in the United States, raising the profile of the Republic of Korea and setting an example of Korean strength and resilience. Many Koreans called us foreign whores and ridicule us, but we are truly Korean patriots.

After the Korean War into the early 1960s, there were not many jobs for women, especially uneducated women in South Korea. There was no factory work. The only real opportunities for many women were jobs as housekeepers, waitresses, or sex workers near US military bases.

I feel incredibly blessed with the opportunities I was given. At the age of sixteen, I was wandering the streets alone without a home or family. Yet miraculously, I became a ROK soldier and was even allowed to finish my high school education. That gave me the chance to get a well-paying job in the US military. I have made Minnesota my home for many years and have lived a good life here.

I know a Korean woman in the United States who is a church deaconess. When she was seventeen years old, she worked as a cabaret dancer and pub waitress. She worked very hard to take care of her family, including her siblings. At one point, her brother cut her hair short and locked her up at home to stop her from working this job. She was able to escape and return to work, sending money to her mother to feed her hungry family. Even though she was younger than her brother, she supported her family throughout her life. The family's survival was on her shoulders.

Today, she lives with her two daughters and looks after them and her grandchildren. She is a strong woman living an honest life. She says she will live to the end of her life in the house of her daughters. Her daughters are also very proud and grateful for their mother.

On my first day working at the base in Waegwan, my boss, the master sergeant, told me, "Miss Kim, there is a lot of theft on this base. You must do a very thorough search of all the employees as they leave."

When people came to the main gate, I had to check for their pass cards, search their bags, and frisk them. Most of the employees hated this, and who could really blame them? Many of them concealed their displeasure, but some were openly disgusted with me, especially when I frisked them. Some of the kinder women would willingly open their handbag so I could do my job more easily.

One of the more stressful interactions was with some of the housekeepers who had fluorescent bulbs, toilet paper, and other miscellaneous objects inside their large hanboks. As they walked to the gate, you could see them walking very strangely. It was an odd sort of walk as they tried to conceal all the things that they were hiding under their outfits. I smiled but was embarrassed. I remember not knowing what to do in this situation. In the end, I decided that they were not stealing anything expensive or important like machine parts. Red-faced, I just waved them through the gate. The women walked through the gate, laughing and thanking me.

I later found out, after I no longer worked at the base, that people often avoided the main gate while I was on guard duty. The other security guards would accept bribes to let people pass—but that did not work for me. Back then, a black market for American goods existed. Lots of Koreans would pay for things smuggled off the base. I was not interested in any of it. Perhaps I was too naive at the time. Every day, I was given a ride home in a military police Jeep. In my five years working there, I never smuggled any American goods off the base.

The Korea of the 1960s was a country that was rebuilding. Eighty percent of the infrastructure was destroyed by the Korean War. Most Koreans were struggling with poverty and looked to get money any way that they could.

John, my now ex-husband and the father of my two sons, was an American military officer. He became my boss, the provost marshal. During my time at the base, he was the fourth person to hold that position.

The provost marshal that preceded him was a very formal, gruff, middle-aged man with a deep voice. When he was sent back to the United States, we all anxiously awaited his replacement.

Then, on a winter day in 1968, a quiet, young second lieutenant arrived as the new provost marshal. To my surprise, on his first day he was carrying a copy of *Beneath the Wheel* by Hermann Hesse, a German author I loved. I had never had a boss that shared my love of literature.

The previous provost marshals were always inviting Korean women from the village outside the back gate to their office. I would often have to serve the women coffee. These were men who had wives and families back in the United States.

But this single, young provost marshal was different than the rest. During his first month of duty, he would have me accompany him on visits to a nearby orphanage. One time, while we were visiting, a young girl had an epileptic seizure. It was total chaos; no one knew what to do. To my surprise, my new boss quickly took out his handkerchief and placed it in the child's mouth to keep her from injuring her teeth or swallowing her tongue. He then worked with an orphanage employee to move the child so she was comfortably lying down. He did it all quite quickly. His actions moved me so much that I became his friend. From then on, special feelings for him started to sprout.

We would sometimes go to the officer's club, where I ate delicious fried chicken for the first time in my life. Sometimes, we would take a US military bus and visit the city. He also took me to the movie theater on the base. We spent time together every weekend. We would even discuss the books we were reading, sharing our thoughts and enjoyment of books that we would read together.

I felt comfortable enough around him that I revealed my true dreams. I told him that I wanted to go to university in the United States. Despite my feelings, I sensed that he was only interested in friendship. He never held my hand when we would spend time together.

One day, he started to open up about himself. He was born in Minnesota. At age fourteen, he entered a Catholic seminary to begin the process of becoming a priest. He went to the Crosier seminary in Onamia for middle school and high school. However, he grew skeptical of the monastic life and was never ordained. He graduated from St. John's University in Minnesota with a bachelor's degree in philosophy.

Instead of becoming a priest, he enlisted in the United States Army and attended officer's school. He was then assigned to the army base in Waegwan, South Korea. He had initially asked to join the Vietnam War. He felt that, as an unmarried person, he should be the one to put himself in danger rather than someone with a family, believing that was a better way to serve his country. I thought he was a very admirable person.

I first heard about the Vietnam War when it began in 1964. As it progressed, it was clear that the United States was at a disadvantage. I watched the war with great concern. Sometimes, I would hear about US soldiers I knew from the base dying in battle in Vietnam. I felt awful for them.

The Vietnam War was the only war in which the United States, one of the world's largest economic and military powers, was defeated.

During this war, many vile and terrible things happened. In hindsight, it was a good thing that John never made it to the Vietnam War.

Eventually, John said to me, "I have not decided yet whether I am going to be ordained as a Catholic priest or not. This is why I have never thought about marriage. However, if you want to allow me to help you to study in the US, I think I can do that."

His pure heart and Christlike love touched me, and I respected him for still considering becoming a priest. Above all, he promised to help me find a way to study in the United States. It was like a dream. I believed at that moment that I truly loved John.

But now when I look back, I wonder if I ever truly loved anyone outside of my children and my grandchildren. With the loss of my parents at such a young age and all the pains and injuries I have endured, I wonder if I can truly trust or love anyone.

I try to be optimistic and do my best every day. I was once afraid of being hurt and focused on surviving, always defending myself like a porcupine. Now, I have had great friendships, like the one I have with Professor Moon. I am grateful for his goodness. Even then, I never completely opened my heart to Professor Moon, with whom I have always been close, like a biological brother. I do not have much love for my real brothers in North Korea because I was young when I was separated from them.

Now in my seventh decade of life, when I look back on the past and think about the end of my life—I do not think I am capable of loving anyone. I only love my sons and my family.

In my life, I have never understood what love is.

CHAPTER FOUR

In the early spring of 1970, John, the US provost marshal, my boss and friend, was discharged from the military and went back home, leaving Waegwan. Before leaving, he helped set up everything for me to study in the United States. He helped me enroll in a women's college in Minnesota through a priest friend of his who sent all the documents I needed for admission. He also helped me find scholarships and an American family that would host me. Five years previously, on October 4, 1965, President Lyndon Johnson signed the 1965 Immigration Act that went into effect two-plus years later, on July 1, 1968. This law opened the door to increased immigration to the United States, particularly for people from Latin American, Asian, and African nations. This began a new chapter of Korean immigration to the United States.

In a speech during the signing, President Johnson explained that the bill was one of the most important acts of his administration and that it "corrects a cruel and enduring wrong in the conduct of the American Nation." Senators Robert and Edward Kennedy also attended the signing. Their brother, the late President John F. Kennedy, had also been a big supporter of immigration reform. The bill abolished the unfair and racist national origins quota system and opened the door for new immigrants of all races and ethnicities to come to the United States.

In many ways, this was a continued expression of the ideals that Martin Luther King Jr. had proclaimed in his "I Have a Dream" speech on August 28, 1963. It began with Kennedy's efforts to pass a Civil Rights Act before his assassination in November of 1963. President

Johnson worked to preserve Kennedy's legacy and pushed for the passage of a civil rights bill in the US Congress. Once passed in 1964, certain types of discrimination previously accepted became illegal in public facilities, workplace employment, and elections. While the law was created with Black Americans in mind, these changes also improved the status of other minority groups.

As such, the Civil Rights Act of 1964 and the Immigration Act of 1965 were critically important for minority immigrant populations in the United States. It is because of this that I have deep respect and gratitude for the actions of Dr. Martin Luther King, Jr., President John F. Kennedy, and President Lyndon B. Johnson.

In 1970, a rule in Korea was that students going to study abroad had to have already attended two years of University in Korea before they could go. The travel agent's office I was working with in Korea was helping me to get this restriction waived so I could still study abroad. I nervously awaited the outcome of my application.

But then a notorious scandal occurred in Korean society that put everything in flux. A woman named Jeong In-suk was found dead in the backseat of her car with a gunshot wound in her head and one in her chest. It was a big story in the newspaper, and it became more and more scandalous with every passing day. She had been a mistress of a powerful politician. In the investigation, the police found she had a notebook with contact information for high-ranking dignitaries and a special passport and visa issued only to high-ranking officials. She had used these credentials to easily travel in and out of the United States. For months, the news press and the Korean people were trading gossip about all the notorious things she did.

Unbelievably, this event that had nothing to do with my life became the spark that lit the fire that burned down any chance that I would be able to study in the United States. Because of the ease with which she had been able to bribe officials to travel in and out of the country, bureaucrats began to tighten up travel restrictions to avoid further scandal and hide their previous wrongdoings. This meant that my application for a student visa was denied.

How very much I resented this woman I had never met! I had become so desperate to leave Korea that now I just wanted to die. No one understood what a terrible place Korea was to me at the time. I longed to leave Korea and go to the United States. Many years later, I did get to study in the United States, eventually graduating from the University of Minnesota as a single mother with two children.

Again, I felt myself resenting my father so deep in my heart. Whenever doors closed in front of me, I had a renewed hatred for my father for deserting me, and I would raise my fist up to him in defiance. Every time I fell, I thought to myself, no one would come to help me.

I also found myself thinking about that day when I was sixteen and I was kicked out of my aunt's house. I remember being very hungry, needing a Korean meal with rice to eat and get energy to face my problems. Ever since I was very young, I have always turned to a Korean meal with rice whenever I was in distress. This is how I have lived and endured.

I was worried because I was also jobless. I had left my well-paying job at the army base because I thought I was leaving to study abroad. I started to panic as the reality of my situation came over me.

I immediately sent John a telegram and told him everything. I told him that I was desperate because I could not go to America to study. I found out that John had decided not to become ordained as a priest. Against his mother's wishes, he returned to Korea at the end of June to marry me and bring me to the United States. On July 2, 1970, we had a small wedding ceremony at the Catholic church in Waegwan, South Korea. My aunt had hastily arranged everything.

The evening before the wedding, John went out with an officer who worked with him at the army base. He got very drunk and came home very late. He was sick all night, vomiting and moaning.

I have no strong memories of the next day, our wedding day. I do not really remember the ceremony, and I threw away the photos because our faces looked stoic and sad, as if we were attending a funeral.

A few days after the wedding, I asked John about that night he got drunk and sick. He said his officer friend was rebuking him for coming back to Korea and marrying a "native" girl. He told him that he should just go home and forget about the wedding. This was an officer who I also knew, who was always very sweet to me, smiling kindly with his soft white face whenever he encountered me. I was surprised by this two-faced racism.

Now, after living in the United States for fifty years, I have met a lot of people exactly like that white officer—people from all walks of life. Even the office of the presidency is no stranger to this kind of racism. America is passing through dark times, struggling with its racist legacy. At that time, I was unaware that this officer's behavior was just the tip of a massive iceberg of racism that I would experience in American white society.

Where I worked on the army base in the provost marshal's office, I did not see a lot of Black soldiers or other people of color. In those years, I saw lots of soldiers processed through the criminal investigation department, drunk and belligerent soldiers, soldiers who committed manslaughter and even murder on Korean civilians, soldiers who stole expensive equipment and supplies from the army base. Virtually all these criminals were white soldiers.

I worked on the US army base, but my only understanding of discrimination was the pain I suffered as a child of a communist in Korean society. I had never even thought about the idea of racism. When I heard John's story, I remembered that I had seen the word "native" somewhere.

While working on the base, I would sometimes do work with the criminal investigation department, working on cases for the provost marshal's office. Korean investigators in the office were dedicated to international marriage cases. Much of the paperwork I did was about international marriages that they were investigating. The file would have the name of a "native" Korean woman seeking to marry an American soldier, along with her past activities, family background, and other miscellaneous details. The marriage documents were attached with transcripts of interviews conducted with the woman's family and neighbors. I always felt embarrassed on behalf of these women, and now I felt shame as I was becoming one of them.

Korean society had a negative view of Korean women who dated or married United States soldiers. When Korean colleagues at the base first found out that John and I were spending time together, they stopped calling me "Miss Kim" and started referring to me as a "GI bride."

One day, a middle-aged Korean employee, who did various tasks for the provost marshal office, whom the US soldiers called "House Boy," told me, "Miss Kim, you live with the provost marshal. Now you are a GI bride."

I was astonished by this and scolded him. "Excuse me? How can you say that to me? You know I live next to the Catholic monastery with my aunt."

But he continued to argue with me. "Don't make excuses. Everyone knows it, even your security guard boss, Mr. Choi, knows about it."

I was really upset! I was an innocent young woman who lived with her aunt, worked hard during the week, and went to church on Sundays—but just because I was friends with John, this man was humiliating me.

My house was not like those outside the back gate, designed for Korean women to entertain GIs with their American double beds and pink sheets. When John and I would go out, we went to the theater or ate delicious fried chicken at the officer's club or read a book together. That was it! John had not even made up his mind about the priesthood at that time.

During those times, working for the US military was seen as a hindrance for a Korean woman looking to marry a good Korean man. Korean matchmakers avoided women working at the base and were reluctant to help us. The stigma was even worse for Korean women at the base wanting to marry an American soldier. Koreans would single them out, calling them "Yankee's whores" or "GI brides." Korean women feared people's thoughts and judgment. I did too.

I was already an orphan and a bbal-gang-i. I served in the Korean Women's Army and had to go to night school. Now I was a GI bride too? I felt persecuted and exposed like Hester Prynne, but with multiple scarlet letters.

I appreciated having John's support. It made it easier to ignore the others' finger-pointing. I considered myself very lucky to be able to leave South Korea and move to the United States.

One Sunday after we were married, John and I went to a Catholic church for mass in Seoul. The priest refused to offer me communion after providing it for John. I was in disbelief. He treated me like I was a foreigner's whore rather than a married woman in the eyes of the church. I grumbled and called him a fake priest. John was angry and said a few choice words to the priest, but it all meant nothing, especially because the priest did not understand any English.

In Korea at the time, if you were a young Korean woman holding a US soldier's hand as you walked down the street, everyone thought of you as a Yankee whore. People would glare at us with contemptuous eyes. We are lucky that they did not start throwing stones.

Those of us who married American soldiers, women like me, had a lot of psychological wounds. Koreans considered our children "half-breeds." When I came to the United States, many Korean immigrants in Minnesota felt the same way about women like me. I really wanted to come to the United States, so I was fine with it.

I had received much ridicule and experienced much shame growing up in South Korea because of my communist father. I lived in such misery because my father abandoned me in favor of his communist ideas. How could my father, who had really adored me, the man who was responsible for his family, make that kind of stupid choice? Was the communist ideal more important to my father than the safety and welfare of his family? How could he have been reckless as a father and a husband? I hated my father from the depths of my heart. A famous radio announcer that was on the air throughout my childhood would shout anticommunist and anti–North Korean slogans on the air every day in her sharp, high voice. It was a reminder of everything my father had done. I wanted to forget the sound of her voice and everything about North Korea. I wanted to get away from all of it.

Finally, when I had a chance to go to the United States, I jumped at it. This was my goal, my dream from when I first started working with the army. I was finally going to get out of this tortured existence in Korea.

In my first month of marriage in Waegwan, I became pregnant with my first son, Chris. When John heard about my pregnancy, he was not happy. He was afraid and told me to have an abortion. This request, from a person who had studied to become a Catholic priest, was surprising and upsetting. My aunt, who was living with us, became very angry when she heard this. "My God! How could you say such a thing! Did you not study to become a priest?" Her eyes filled with the tears as she turned to John. "You know I was not able to have my own child. How can you say such an awful thing right in front of me? What if something goes wrong and you never have another chance to have a baby. If you don't want this baby, then leave it here with me! I will raise your baby, and the two of you can go off to America. Disgusting! How does this happen!"

My aunt intervened, and my baby was safe. John returned to the United States while I remained in Seoul and took care of the immigration process. The night before John left, he handed me twenty-five US dollars and said, "You will need some cash when you land in the United States." That twenty-five dollars was all I brought to America.

***

It was Thanksgiving Day 1970 when I arrived in the United States with twenty-five dollars and my big hopes and dreams. I arrived at the Minneapolis–St. Paul airport in Minnesota. John was waiting for me when I landed. It was freezing and snowy. As we drove to our apartment, everything seemed quite bleak.

November in Minnesota is windy and cold. Everything was covered in snow. The landscape was flat. The snow kept blowing and falling across the road as we drove. Because John's family had been against the marriage, no one else greeted me when I arrived.

The landscape was white and bright in this flat, snowy city, with hardly a hill or low ridge. Matchbox-like apartments dotted the snowy landscape along the endless snow-covered road. It reminded me of Marc Chagall's painting of his home village. I began a meager American life here.

John turned the car into a parking lot beside a wide street by a strange-looking, old building—our apartment. When I entered the living room, it was completely empty with no furniture, not even a small chair. Bedsheets covered the windows and when the wind blew, they made a flapping noise. In the middle of a small bedroom, a single shabby mattress was on the floor covered in dirty blankets. I was a little shocked and even embarrassed. Soon, I changed my mindset and resolved to love this home. I was determined to make my hopes and dreams come true in this American land that I loved so much.

A few days later, my husband's brother came to the apartment with a worn-out old sofa. John's brother had left the priesthood and moved out of the church rectory. He had been a Catholic priest. From that day on, I lived together in this old, cramped apartment with my husband and his brother.

The Minnesota winter of 1970 was bitterly cold. I was pregnant with my first child, and I saw my life beginning in the United States as one of poverty. I was going to give birth in a few months; however, with my bulging stomach, I was also cleaning house and cooking for two men.

I believe John married me only to help bring me to the United States—and thought that was enough. He did not give me a wedding ring, nor did we have a honeymoon. We had no plans for our future together.

There were no mountains where we lived. I was quite lonely, and I yearned for the mountains of Korea. I was in this faraway place, Minnesota. Here is where I had to prepare to give birth to my first child. I came to the United States in the 1970s. It had been only a few years after Dr. Martin Luther King Jr. and the Civil Rights Movement had worked to change things for people of color in America. There was still a lot of racism in America at that time, and even today.

My husband's family was no exception, especially my mother-in-law, a German American. She was a devout Catholic and had wanted her two boys to become priests. Her older son had left the priesthood because of a relationship with a woman. Her second son, John, who had been studying for so long, gave up on the priesthood before receiving ordination. Now he was bringing home a woman, me, from an uncivilized country. She did not like me—or at least the idea of me. Before John went to Korea to marry me, she begged John's friend to find a local white girl to introduce to him. There I was, living with two of her sons, the one that became a priest and left and the one that married me. When I finally arrived in the US, it was some time before I met my mother-in-law.

John had attended high school at a monastery and studied for the priesthood all through his time at university. I feel like he never really learned how to be a good husband or how to care for a family or a household. He did not have a full-time job. One cold, snowy day that winter, his old car, the only vehicle we had, completely broke down. That car did not get fixed, even after the birth of my son the following spring. That dirty, old, broken-down car just sat in the corner of the apartment parking lot forever.

It was the night of April 11, 1971. I had cooked dinner, and the three of us were eating. Suddenly, I experienced severe pain, and I knew the baby was ready to come out. I had to go to the hospital. Of course, our old, broken-down car did not work—and John called the police.

Suddenly, I was in significant pain, and I was screaming, so the police called an ambulance, which turned out to be expensive. I arrived at the hospital in this ambulance with its loud siren. In the United States, you need medical insurance to pay for giving birth in a hospital, but we did not have any. The ambulance ride, the hospital stay, and the doctor visits amounted to a considerable amount of money that we had to pay in medical bills later.

Once I was at the hospital, it felt as if the pain was going to last forever, but after a long period of labor, I finally gave birth to a boy. When the nurse placed the baby in my arms, I did as my aunt had instructed and checked his hands and feet to make sure he had ten fingers and ten toes. I saw them all wiggling about, and I was happy and relieved. Because we had no insurance, we decided to leave St. Joseph's Hospital in Saint Paul that day.

The doctor told me that my son was a big baby who weighed over nine pounds. The nurses laughed and said that he would be able to walk on his own when we left the hospital. In the hospital, people were talking about the tiny Asian mother who gave birth to a giant baby. I had bled a lot during the birth, and the nurse bathed me with cold water. I remember shivering from the cold. Because I did not stay in the hospital, I did not receive any real aftercare.

If I were in Korea, I would have rested in a warm room for days after the birth. I would have been well cared for by relatives and fed seaweed soup every day for many months. In truth, there was no sea-weed soup back at the apartment; in fact, there was little to eat. I did not eat well, even though I had just given birth to my first son.

My precious first son was born. My aunt, who was in Korea and who had saved my son, was delighted and rejoiced like a general re-turning home after winning a war. My son's eyes were gray at first but gradually turned to a greenish-brown, hazel color. I was so excited that my baby's eyes were so beautiful, and I often gazed into my son's eyes. That is when all my worries would melt away, staring into my son's beautiful eyes. Then I was happy.

I did not get good aftercare, and I felt very stressed. I had terrible nightmares every night. One day, I realized I could not cook and clean for two men anymore. I told my husband that I would like to go and live with my mother-in-law in the countryside.

There was very little postpartum care for me there either. During the month I spent at my in-laws' home, my mother-in-law would not let me rest. Instead, she taught me how to cook various American dishes. She made me learn how to bake cookies and cakes. I was on my feet almost all day. I did, in fact, learn a lot about Western cooking. My mother-in-law gave me a Betty Crocker cookbook, which I used for a long time. I still love that book.

One day, I went to breastfeed my baby as my aunt had taught me. My mother-in-law shouted in amazement and scolded me for pulling out my breast like an uncivilized woman. She made me sit alone in a chair in the kitchen corner. She said no one should see me breastfeed my baby. Regardless, I didn't breastfeed for long because my mother-in-law was trying to wean my son and have him take bottles instead. She would feed him bottles, and I could not feed him my breast milk. My breasts became overloaded with milk and always hurt. My mother-in-law was not very kind to me—but she adored her first grandson, my son, very much.

In 1971, not many Koreans or even Asians lived in Minnesota. The only Korean food store was near the university and very expensive. The one Korean restaurant was small, and the food was not very good. I had really wanted to leave Korea, but now I missed and yearned for the comforts of my own country. I had to endure the idea of living every day in this strange place.

Luckily, our first child was very healthy. When I saw my baby son growing up and getting bigger day by day, my loneliness and fear seemed to fade. I had always felt very alone in the world—but now I had this new life that had come from my own body. He was so precious and essential to me.

I wanted to be with my baby boy every moment. Everything about him looked beautiful and precious to me. We still had a difficult life; John did not have a full-time job, and my mother-in-law helped by making homemade baby food for us. She always remarked, "Well, I can't let my grandson starve," as she filled our refrigerator with jars of homemade baby food.

After the month I spent in my in-law's house out in the country, John and I would sometimes go back to visit them and some other relatives. It always made me feel lonely. I missed the Korean country-side and the beautiful mountains.

It was the summer following that first harsh winter. We would often drive out into the country to visit John's parents. On the drive, I would see stretches of flat open fields and sometimes a seemingly end-less cornfield. At times we would stop and visit a farm run by some of John's relatives. I would walk alone through the cornfield until it was just me and the cornfield under the vast blue sky. I would hear a sharp wind blow through the corn—and I could feel the beat of my lonely heart in the sound of the shivery breeze.

Because we had a baby without proper insurance, the hospital and maternity expenses became apparently insurmountable debts. We needed many things just to live, and yet we were poor.

I could not understand John. When John was a provost marshal at the army base in Waegwan, the base's commander in chief praised his excellent leadership. He told John that if he remained in the mili-tary, he would be promoted to captain. When he rejected their offer to return to the US, I believed that he must have had a plan for our future. When I joined him in Minnesota, he did not even have a steady job, just the occasional part-time job. He wanted to use his GI bill and go to grad school.

Eventually, I was able to find a job as a keypunch operator. I had learned this skill while I was in Korea. My son was a year old, and we found a babysitter who was a caretaker of the Catholic church near our apartment. Once I had a fixed income, I began to pay for our living expenses and pay off our debt. I also felt much more comfortable sending money to my aunt in Korea to cover her living expenses. I also began researching and applying for US citizenship so I could someday bring my aunt to the United States.

Early every morning, I would put my son in a baby carriage and bring him to the babysitter's house. I took a bus to work for a big company called General Mills in the city of Minneapolis. One day, when I was picking up my son on my way home, his caregiver laughed and said, "Your son is so smart. Even though he is still a baby, he knows precisely when you are coming to pick him up and always goes to wait at the door just before you arrive."

My favorite part of the day was after work when I would put my son in his baby carriage and walk home. When my son saw my face, he would feel safe and secure, then almost always dirty his diaper in the baby carriage. I would gaze lovingly at the face of my son. Even the diaper smell seemed sweet to me. When we got home, I would give him a bath. When I think about it now, it is still a small precious memory that makes me smile and laugh.

I had started working in early spring. By fall, I had enough money to be able to buy a car. Then I was able to change jobs to work for a trucking company that paid a higher salary. I started to work the night shift, and I would leave my son with John, who had returned to school. I was happy that I did not have to leave our son with a babysitter. The cost was reduced, and my son would get to spend time with his father. For nearly ten years, I would take jobs where I worked nights.

Later, I worked as a bartender for a long time. Every night, my colleagues at the trucking company would talk about becoming bartenders. They said that people could earn twice as much money as what we were making there. When I heard that, I immediately visited a bartending school near my job. I asked the school to guarantee that I would be able to get a job that paid at least four dollars an hour or else refund half my tuition. When they accepted this arrangement, I signed up for classes.

The bartending school was near my work, making it easy to take classes. Over the next few months, I learned a lot. The instructors praised me for my cocktail-making skills. However, once my training was complete, it was not easy to get a job. The owner of the school eventually got me hired at his mother-in-law's restaurant. But the wage was only $3.50, so I went back to the school and received a refund for half of the tuition. As time passed, my income increased, and with tips I was indeed receiving twice as much money as I had previously, just as my former work colleagues had said. During this time, I was finally granted US citizenship after a three-year wait. Now that I was a citizen, I brought my aunt to Minnesota.

We had moved around a lot before then. John had frequently switched schools, deciding what to do. He enrolled in the University of Minnesota in the fall before my aunt came. We decided to move into an apartment in student-family housing. Our move-in date was later than expected, so we had to move out and temporarily store our things in a friend's garage. On a cold winter day, we eventually moved into the student apartment. Then, a month later, John decided to leave that school. On another cold, winter day, we moved again. We had moved three times in five months. I was exhausted from my work and from my life, but I continued to work hard, holding out hope that John would become a university professor.

Many more men were bartenders than women. It was often difficult physical work, and we had to stand all the time. We had to bend down repeatedly to move things in and out of the refrigerator. We had to restock the rail (behind the bar) with bottles of alcohol to use for cocktails. We had to continually wash and dry cocktail glasses and thick, heavy beer glasses. I had gotten pregnant again, but my work was very physical, and I had a miscarriage.

John had enrolled in graduate school in Wisconsin, and because the school was a long drive away, it was hard for us to see each other. John seemed to spend a lot of time with his female classmates and friends. One time, he called me at two in the morning because he was at the dormitory of his friend, a Japanese woman, who was homesick. Another time, a friend with whom he carpooled called asking where he was. John had not come to pick him up yet. I found out later that he was late because he was waiting to pick up another friend, a Taiwanese woman, and that she had overslept. I wondered why he was willing to go to these extremes to help these women when we hardly had time to see each other.

Later, we bought a house. John stubbornly insisted we could only afford this small, cramped house with a giant lawn. It had a leaky roof, and we would have to put out buckets on the floor every time it rained.

Many windows were cracked, and when the glass on the front door broke, we covered it in cardboard. It had a few rooms and no basement. Dark mold was often on the walls, and sometimes I would find mealworms and bugs when I opened the rice cooker.

One day, after my aunt had come to live with us, she asked me why my husband drank a lot. I told her that she was mistaken because he could not drink a lot if he was studying for school. I thought nothing of it.

I would work at the bar from 5:00 p.m. until 2:00 a.m. At 1:00 a.m., I would shoo the customers out, and then I would have a lot of things to do for the next day. We would restock the coolers with beer. Then we would throw out all the empty liquor bottles and replace them with new bottles from storage. Next, we would wash all the beer mugs and glasses and put them on the drying stand. Finally, we had to count all the money earned that day and put it in the safe. I was usually able to leave the restaurant at around 2:00 a.m. Sometimes, the other bartenders would get drunk after closing and not make it into work the next day. I often worked their shifts for them to make extra money. When I got home, I would be dead tired.

I worked as a bartender for about ten years. During that time, I noticed that Americans drink a lot of alcohol. Even in the middle of the day, they would order cocktails like Manhattans or martinis and go back to work. Of course, many people would stop by the bar after work too. Every bar was full of people, even at one in the morning. After working as a bartender, I developed a lifelong habit of never over-drinking. People make mistakes and are vulnerable when under the influence of alcohol. As a foreigner and a non-native English speaker, I felt like I had to be extra careful.

Dealing with drunks was not easy. Sometimes, I had to deal with racist customers and coworkers. If I cut off a drunk customer, they would sometimes tell me I was stupid and that I should "go back to China." Mostly it came from terrible men, but women could be just as bad.

After I had a miscarriage, I felt tired all the time. I quit working at night. I got a job bartending at a golf club with an upper middle-class clientele. With no tips, my income was less, but it was much more comfortable work.

One time, a bartender there, a middle-aged white guy, who often referred to me as his "little gook." I had never heard this term before, so it confused me. One morning, I asked John what it meant. Suddenly, John was furious and stood up from his seat. He drove me to work that day and came inside and shouted at the bartender. "You bastard! How dare you call my wife a gook! Apologize to her now!" The bartender was shocked and apologized to me immediately and repeatedly.

That was when I found out that *gook* was (and still is) a derogatory, racist term used to describe people from East and Southeast Asia. My sons and I have all experienced people calling us chinks or gooks.

When my son was in elementary school, a blonde woman showed up at our home and shouted at me about my son punching her son and giving him a bloody nose. I apologized at first and told her I would talk to him, then meet her later at the school.

But when I asked my son about it, he told me that this boy had been calling him a chink. He said that he usually put up with it because he was Korean and not Chinese. That day, the boy had pulled a chair from under him, and he hit his head on the floor. My son got angry and punched him in the face. I reassured my son and went to school to tell his teacher what had happened. The angry blonde woman did not visit our house again.

Another word about my ex-mother-in-law—she was a German American woman. After she graduated high school, she immediately got married and spent her life being a good housewife and raising a family. As I mentioned earlier, she was a racist, but it was often a subtle, soft-spoken racism. She especially seemed to have an antipathy toward Black people, but I felt it too as an Asian. She was blunt and condescending to me, but she was very sweet to the white wife of John's younger brother. They were very gregarious to one another. As

Americans sometimes do, they would call each other by their first names, not as "mother-in-law" or "daughter-in-law."

When I told her the story of my parents, my mother-in-law bluntly told me that they were irresponsible parents for abandoning their child. I did not argue with her.

A particular incident that happened in her home has always stuck with me. When my aunt came to Minnesota from Korea, my mother-in-law invited us for dinner. We happily drove the ninety minutes to get to John's parents' house.

When we arrived, my mother-in-law's brother, his wife, and their two children were also there for some reason. Eight chairs were at the dinner table, and my mother-in-law had arranged for herself, my father-in-law, my husband, my son, her brother, and his wife and two children to sit at the table. Then, on a little side table in the kitchen, she had arranged places for my aunt and me to sit. It was a little Formica table with a pale florescent bulb for light. There we sat, finishing our meal quietly, separate from the rest of the group.

When the meal was complete, my aunt stood up and requested we return home. Others were still sitting around the table talking. We said our goodbyes to my mother-in-law and father-in-law, then left the house.

On the car ride home, my aunt said, "I have something to say to your husband. Can you translate it for me? Ask him, Do Americans treat their in-laws this way? How could you make your mother-in-law eat in the kitchen like that? Are we not part of the family? What a humiliating experience! Ask your husband. Did he eat well? I will never set foot in that house ever again." True to her word, she never visited John's parent's house at any point.

A few years ago, my ex-mother-in-law died of old age. When her estate went up for sale, my youngest son jokingly asked if I wanted them to get her kitchen table so I could take an axe to it. I would never waste my energy on such a thing—but I appreciate that my sons understood the pain that this caused.

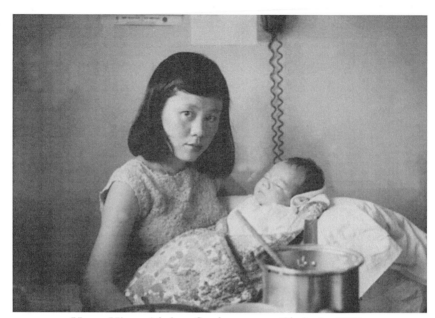

Hyon Kim with her firstborn son, Chris, in 1971
Fridley, MN
Credit: Photo Collection of Hyon Kim

CHAPTER FIVE

Ever since I first came to the United States, I could not rest. I kept looking ahead and running forward. After working hard for more than ten years, my body and mind were exhausted. But I was also exhausted by the dreams and expectations I had about my husband. I sometimes felt like my husband was just a third son for me to support. He was interested in getting a master's degree, but he had a difficult time getting into a program because of his college grades. He eventually made it into a psychology program at a small school in Wisconsin.

It never seemed like he was studying very hard. He seemed to enjoy drinking and hanging out with friends more than studying. I eventually gave up on my dream of John becoming a professor, the same way his mother gave up her dream of him becoming a priest. But without that, my biggest problem was that I did not know what my dream was.

After working as a bartender for over nine years, I became very tired of this lifestyle. The last place I bartended was in a fancy hotel restaurant near my home. The hotel had three bars. I worked hard there to feed my children.

One day, when I was working at the piano bar, a very drunk guest picked a fight with me. He started shouted vulgarities, and he was getting on my last nerve. I held up an empty bottle and said, "If I hear another dirty word come out of your mouth, I am going to throw this bottle at you!"

He continued to shout more vulgar words—and I threw it at him. Fortunately for him, the bottle missed his head, but he became very angry and called the police. When the police came, none of the other customers took the side of the vulgar drunk, and the bar manager worked quickly to resolve the situation.

After the incident, I quietly followed the manager to her office, expecting to quit or get fired. Instead, she put me at ease and said something surprising. She told me that the hotel needed an honest bartender like me. She said they had been rotating me across the three bars because they could get a clear sense of how much money each bar was making. Management would plan and budget based on my shifts because they knew I was not skimming tips or intentionally miscounting inventory. She made it clear that they did not want me throwing bottles at customers, but she also gave me a raise.

I understood what she meant about the staff being dishonest. The bar always had a lot of customers every day. Sometimes, I would make dozens of cocktails all at once for a waitress, who was thinking she could slide a little extra cash my way so I would not count every drink at the register. She was wrong and I became tired of her behavior. One waitress was a medical student, and I told her, "No matter how sick I was, if I go to the hospital and you were the doctor, I would walk out. How could I entrust my life to a person as dishonest as you?"

All sorts of shady things happened at the bar. We often dealt with drunk people who would drink late into the night. But even many of the bartenders would secretly drink while they were working. I remember one bartender who was a little too fond of drinking tequila on the job and there would be missing bottles when I did inventory at the end of the day. Another bartender at the main bar also worked as a bookie, taking bets at the bar.

I had grown tired of this job and lifestyle. I clearly did not want to work as a bartender—so much so that I threw that bottle at a customer. I was tired of dealing with drunks. And at home, I was also tired of dealing with my husband. I felt like I had nothing to hope for in my life.

My life was such a mess. I was constantly fighting with my husband over the littlest things. I would almost have rather heard rumors that he was having an affair. My husband seemingly did not care about the leaking roof or broken windows or the moldy walls in our house. But he took the time to cut down branches from our backyard trees and bring firewood to his friend and drink wine with her.

John's penchant for drinking continued to be a problem. He once told me that many of the seminary students at his university would frequently get drunk and pass out. When I thought about that, I thought these students must endure many difficulties to drive them to drink so recklessly. I thought it was perhaps impossible to follow this path without the help of the Holy Spirit. My husband had gone to seminary since middle school, following his mother's wish. He graduated university as a seminary student. He told me that even in middle school, each student had a small tool for self-flagellation in his room.

John studied to be a priest for many years. It was maybe from this training that he turned out to be such a decent and good man. Despite all our fighting, I do believe him to be a good person. I sometimes wonder if he may have just met the wrong woman. I wonder what his life would have been like if he had met a compatible white woman from Minnesota instead of me. I think that maybe he married me not because he was in love with me, but because he wanted to help me.

The summer before we divorced, I had asked my friend's husband and father-in-law, who ran a home-remodeling business, to give me a quote on expanding our home. I was pleased with their estimate and knew that we could afford the monthly payments if we took out a loan to make the changes. Our house was tiny, and I was desperate to remodel it. But John opposed it. At that time, a married woman in the United States needed her husband's signature to get a loan of this type. He never signed the documents, and therefore we never went through with the remodel.

Our house had a spacious backyard, but we had no basement, and the house was tiny. It was too small for a family with two children. Even an older Korean woman once remarked to me that she had never seen a house in the United States that was this small.

Once, in the middle of winter, our dryer stopped working. When we bought the house, the seller gave us the old washer, dryer, stove, and dishwasher for only one hundred dollars—but all of it was old. When the dryer broke, I suggested we get a new one because it was already old, and I had enough money to buy one. But John insisted we borrow a friend's truck and take it to the local technical school where they would repair it for free.

That winter, we had to take our laundry to the laundromat. Minnesota winters are famously cold, and with two children we had a lot of laundry. It was a constant hassle to do this all winter long. When I reflect on it, I wonder why I did not just go out and buy a dryer myself with my own money. Again, John and I were fighting all the time.

We purchased the house in 1975 for $25,000 on a thirty-year mortgage. It was a small house built right after World War II. When my aunt saw our house for the first time, she said, "What kind of thoughtless, narrow-minded person would even build such a small home?"

She did not even know the half of it. The day we signed the purchase agreement, John became so stressed by the amount of debt that he was violently ill for a week, vomiting on and off every day. I think it was at this point that I truly believed that John only married me to help me but never truly loved me or wanted to be with me.

I know that John had many female friends, but I never doubted his fidelity. That was never the reason we got divorced. It was just something I decided one day after yet another one of our terrible fights. I decided it was better to get divorced than to fight every day. I thought I could live in peace without him. We could go our separate ways with our separate futures. Even though the prospect of a future in this foreign country without a husband scared me, I thought it was a better way for happiness for me.

At this point, John had been working as a caseworker at a state prison. He had also finished his long journey to his master's degree. We had been married for ten years when we finally decided to get a divorce.

But during the divorce process, John became my enemy. Because I was working nights, he filed a petition for primary custody of the children. It was because of him that I had worked nights all those years—and now it was being used against me. I quit my job immediately and found a day job at an insurance company as a word-processing administrator. Fortunately, in the end, the court gave me primary custody.

One thing I do regret is not taking my lawyer's advice to get a portion of John's pension. During the divorce process, my lawyer was insistent that I was owed that money because of the times that I worked while he was in school. I refused this suggestion, and my lawyer quit in protest. I ended up signing the final papers without legal representation. Sometimes, I think I am too naive and trusting, especially with money.

Even though I felt that he did not love me, I did appreciate that John brought me to the United States. I did not want his future income—and I did not understand this American system and culture that wanted me to take that from him. But when I think about it, for the sake of my two sons, I perhaps should have listened to that attorney.

We finally signed the divorce papers. John and I were no longer husband and wife. I thought it was better that way. I know he did not love me the way a husband loves a wife. When I think of it even now, there has always been an empty place deep in my heart. In my life, I have never truly experienced a loving relationship with any man.

After I divorced John, the first thing I did was get a bank loan to start repairing our small house. I fixed the holes in the roof, the broken windows, and the broken door. I also got rid of all of the unhealthy black mold on the walls. Each wall was cleaned and painted. Then our little house became neat and clean. It was in this clean, very small house that I lived with my two sons.

Many years later, when my youngest son was twenty-five years old, he built a brand-new house on the same property as our small house. He first removed the house where we used to live. Then he built a beautiful four-bedroom house with a basement and a three-car garage for his family. I was thrilled because this was what I had always wished I could do when we were living there. It was a fulfillment of my dream.

From 1975 to 1988, I worked hard to maintain that house, fixing things that were broken, paying down the mortgage. Now a new house has arisen in that place, built by my son and his wife as a home for their family. Even today, my youngest son lives there with his wife and three children.

Once, when I was living in that house with my two sons, I had a dream. In that dream, I was holding my two sons' hands while we watched our house catch fire and burn down. According to Korean dream interpretation, this dream means that house is a tremendous place of good fortune. I pray that it will continue to be a lucky house for my son and his family for a long, long time.

When I went through the divorce, it was the Korean Catholic church that gave me the deepest wounds. Of course, the Catholic religion itself has conservative views on divorce. Beyond that, the members of the church knew that John had studied to become a priest and was considering being ordained before he met me.

Many members of the Korean American community in Minnesota have a prejudice against women who are married to American soldiers. I experienced this bias firsthand in the Korean Catholic church a few years before my divorce.

One day, the Korean priest asked my son to be an altar boy for mass. My son was attending a local Catholic elementary school at the time, and I had been confirmed in the Catholic church. Additionally, my son's father had studied to become a priest, and he came from a devout Catholic family. I gratefully accepted the priest's request. But then the father of the other altar boy complained to the priest that he could not allow his son to serve as an altar boy with my son. He claimed that my past was suspect, implying that my son and I were somehow not worthy or pure enough.

Besides being completely untrue, this was such an unbelievable thing to be accused of. It left a big wound in my heart. I had lost my entire family because of my communist father. Now my sons were the only family I had in the world. How could they treat them that way? After that, I stopped attending the Korean Catholic church and joined another non-Korean church in my community.

I divorced John because he did not love me, and I grew tired of his harsh indifference toward our life together. We fought relentlessly every day when we were married. However, I always felt heartbroken and regretful about my divorce. But my sons have told me to never regret my divorce—they know it was the right thing to do. Thanks to them, I have stopped feeling guilty about it. John has remarried a long-time friend that he had known since before our divorce.

I have long been thinking of the lasting wounds of my broken childhood. I am now guilty of giving a broken home to my sons. I honestly believe that Korea's matchmaking system is a good idea. You can research a person's family background and other traits to make sure there is compatibility before dating and marrying. I know that I am not a good prospect for marriage. I would get a failing grade as a bride in the same way my father would get a failing grade as a husband and father. After the divorce, I was working at the insurance company during the day. Then, at thirty-five-years old, I finally decided to go to school. As I searched for the right program, I found myself visiting an advising center at the University of Minnesota. Within the university system are twenty-nine colleges. One was called General College, and it was for students were not qualified for the other schools due to personal circumstances or lack of previous education—people like me. The advising center that I was at was called the HELP (Higher Education for Low-Income Parents) Center, and it was designed to help low-income women with children to attend school. Discovering this place was the answer to my prayers.

I was not fully qualified to attend university, and I thought I was too old. I was scared and very nervous. I met with a counselor named Caroline and told her that I wanted to come to school here, but I had two children and was going to turn forty soon.

Caroline smiled broadly at me and said, "Whether you go to school or not, you will still turn forty—so you may as well attend school."

I asked if I should attend a two-year college.

She said, "I think you are going to graduate from a four-year college." I was excited and happy listening to Caroline.

Many years later, in 1994, I was elected to the Board of Regents at the University of Minnesota. The people at the HELP Center were elated. Caroline and Bev, another advisor and friend, were happy. They hugged me and told me that not only had I graduated with a four-year degree, but I was also their new boss. But as they put it, I was everybody's boss at the university.

Bev also worked at the HELP Center. She was the director and welcomed me on that first day. When she found out I had an administrative job at an insurance company, she immediately put me in touch with their administrator Cheryl to interview for a position at the HELP Center. She said she wanted me working there while I was in school. It felt like a dream! Cheryl interviewed me and immediately hired me to work with her at the HELP Center. Caroline and Bev helped me apply for financial aid and enroll in the work-study program. With their advice, I was able to choose and enroll in the right classes for me. It all worked out very well.

For me, these people were like angels. All of this seemed like a beautiful dream. My dream, which had seemingly gone up in smoke in 1970 after the Jeong In-suk tragedy made it impossible for me to study in the US, was now coming true eleven years later. I was studying at the University of Minnesota, in the United States. But now I was doing it as a middle-aged woman while raising two sons and working nearly full time. It was not easy to find time to study. It was a struggle every day. I even took classes in the summer, with no break for me.

Every evening, I would make food for my children and ask their father to watch them. Then I would go straight to the library. I was working thirty hours each week, studying, and raising my children. I was very busy. About once a year, I would become so fatigued and overtired that I would get physically sick.

I began to realize how unprepared I really was for college. I seemed to have forgotten everything that I had learned in high school. I could not remember anything; simple arithmetic was sometimes difficult. I had to start over, relearning algebra and trigonometry.

The United States has a long, bloodstained history of racism. But there are also places like the Martin Luther King Jr. Center at the University, which assists minority students like me. A very skilled university professor taught classes in beginning mathematics. By taking his classes, I was able to rebuild my knowledge, starting with simple arithmetic, and progress all the way to calculus. Eventually, I even tutored calculus one on one at the HELP Center. I was also promoted from my administrative job to peer counselor. All this was thanks to Bev, Caroline, and Cheryl.

The counselors were a diverse group of Black, Asian, Native American, and Hispanic women, each with an office. My job as a peer counselor was, as a fellow student, to work with single-mother students who were studying while raising a child alone. I worked through various issues with them.

Among other things, I researched success rates of single mothers both in completing college and quality of life after college. Single mothers who completed college reported consistently having higher living standards, higher incomes, and a better quality of life. But unfortunately, many single mothers never completed school. So many of them that came through our program would just drop out and disappear. I do not think it was because these women were not smart. I do not even think it was always because of the difficulties of parenting. I think many of them put their faith in boyfriends or got involved with someone who abused drugs or alcohol.

At American universities, students must study very hard. It can be very difficult to graduate when a student falls behind. This is even harder to navigate when you have children. I had to work while raising my children, but I had to also focus on attending classes and studying.

Every Friday during lunch, we'd hold a session with the single-mother students at the HELP Center, and we would shout slogans about how we were going to limit our distractions and stay celibate like nuns in a convent. "No men until graduation!"

Even today, when I meet with other women I studied with at the time, we laugh and reminisce about how it was difficult, yet it generated so many great memories. When our children had a day off from school, we would bring them to the HELP Center. Sometimes, we would have parties, and we would bring different food from our various cultures to share and feast on together. I especially enjoyed memories of this time with my sons. It may not always be difficult to get into university in the United States, but it takes hard work to graduate. Many students do not finish, dropping out part way through their degrees. I was fortunate that my ex-husband John was willing to look after our sons while I was studying and working. He has always been a good father to our two sons before and after the divorce—his focus was always on them. He did not remarry until they both were adults.

***

I feel fortunate to have immigrated to the United States when I did. Many women and civil rights activists in this country have paved the way so an immigrant woman of color like me could have the opportunities to succeed that I have had. I always feel very grateful to them. The first women's rights convention in the United States was in 1848, in Seneca Falls, New York. This began the long road to women's suffrage, for which American women activists fought hard, culminating in the passage of the Nineteenth Amendment to the US Constitution on August 18, 1920, giving women the right to vote.

Many American women activists worked together with Black abolitionists seeking freedom and justice for all people. In 1865, a full four years after the beginning of the US Civil War that had claimed the lives of nearly 620,000 Americans, Black slaves were finally emancipated in the United States.

In 1870, the Fifteenth Amendment to the Constitution was passed, providing citizens of color the right to vote—which did not result in Black suffrage. Southern states began finding other barriers for Black voters. White supremacist groups like the Ku Klux Klan used terrorist techniques. The most effective method was so-called poll taxes, which were additional fees or requirements for voting that were not explicitly about race, but targeted Black voters.

One example of this was a literacy test, which evaluates the voter's ability to read and write, claiming that a citizen needs to demonstrate a fundamental political and social awareness to be allowed vote. As farmers and former slaves, most Blacks had either no access to or need for a formal education and were of course unable to pass the test. Furthermore, a so-called grandfather clause was included, which exempted uneducated white men whose grandfather or father had voted. As such, this test was created to hinder Black suffrage. While these grandfather clauses were declared unconstitutional in 1915, poll taxes existed well into the 1960s. Oral literacy tests began to be administered, which were still easier for whites to pass and had the added effect of disenfranchising many Spanish-speaking voters in states like Texas.

Not until the Civil Rights Act of 1964, the Voting Rights Act of 1965, and the Twenty-Fourth Amendment in 1964 were these injustices finally addressed in national elections. Then, in 1966, the US Supreme Court declared that poll taxes in state elections were unconstitutional. All of this led to a sharp increase in Black voter turnout.

Rosa Parks, a Black woman in her early forties, was working in Montgomery, Alabama. On December 1, 1955, Rosa Parks boarded the bus and sat in an empty seat in one of the first rows of the "colored" section toward the back of the bus. However, because the bus was crowded and the white-only seats filled up, the driver demanded that she vacate her seat and move further back to accommodate additional white passengers. At the time, the front seats of the bus were only for white people—and Black people had to move if there were too many white people in the white section. But Rosa Parks would not move. The police were called in and arrested her. She was found guilty of disorderly conduct and fined fourteen dollars. She appealed the decision and issued a formal challenge on legal segregation. Her arrest inspired the Montgomery Bus Boycott, a protest during in which African Americans refused to ride city buses in Montgomery, Alabama—a pivotal moment that sparked the Civil Rights Movement. A twenty-six-year-old Black minister who was relatively new to Montgomery heard the news. He began working with local Black leaders to extend the boycott and support this test case. In the end, the boycott lasted 381 days. Blacks were unified in their position, and some white citizens also participated. The minister was the great Dr. Martin Luther King Jr., and this was the beginning of the journey that would see him lead the March for Freedom and make his famous "I Have a Dream" speech in front of the Lincoln Memorial in August of 1963.

Due to the efforts of people like Dr. King, the US Congress passed the 1964 Civil Rights Act. Then, in 1965, a new immigration law was passed that eliminated the historically racially discriminatory immigration policies of the United States. Before the 1965 law, a preference system based on national origins of the current US population was designed to preserve the current racial mix. It favored immigration from northern and western European countries—and severely limited immigrants from southern and Eastern Europe, Africa, Latin America, and Asia.

With the rise of the Civil Rights Movement, the racial biases of the current immigration policy came under attack, and the 1965 Immigration Act was passed. This removed the racist preference system and allowed for more immigration from countries with non-white populations. In many ways, Black people fighting for their civil rights directly helped Koreans like me who wanted to come to the United States.

Sadly, Dr. Martin Luther King Jr. was shot to death by a white man in 1968. Losing his voice was a heartbreaking loss, and the death of this great civil rights activist remains a sad tragedy in American history.

Since then, you can see the results of the civil rights and Women's Rights Movement gradually take shape in the United States. The

Women's Rights Movement from the 1960s to the '80s is often called "second-wave feminism." I felt like I was riding that wave in 1981 when I enrolled at the university at the age of thirty-five.

I was assisted by some great women activists—women who helped and protected other women working hard in school while raising children with little money. These activists were not necessarily out picketing on the street, but they were using their roles as counselors or professors to make it their life's work to help minorities and women. Caroline and Bev are two of those women who were my heroes and my angels.

They helped many women who, like me, had little income, were struggling to study and raise children, and trying to find a way to go to college. They were there every step of the way, helping us find solutions to our economic and academic problems. They paved the way to graduation, showing consistent attention and encouragement every day. If they had not been next to me, I may have given up on that difficult journey to my college degree.

Others supported me as well, especially my two sons. My oldest would often correct my English in my papers. They both still work with me today at our civil engineering company.

Though when I think of my sons, it is often with a sad heart. I feel like the physical and mental abuse that I experienced as a child seeped into my treatment of them, especially when I was sad and lonely. I was often obsessive and stern with them, especially to my older son, forcing them to study hard and treating them very harshly.

In my heart I would think, *You don't understand. This is nothing compared to the pain I experienced. And I am your real mother! You came from me, from my belly.* But I was very hard on them. Despite this, my sons endured it well and have grown into good men.

Because of my past, I was happy that my two sons had much family on their father's side—grandparents, uncles, aunts, cousins, and of course their father, John. On holidays like Thanksgiving, Christmas, and Easter, I would reluctantly allow them to be with their family, even though it meant I was often alone or with others who were not family.

I always found ways to stay busy, but looking back, I have had so many years where I felt desperately lonely.

One winter day, during my fifth and final year of college, I was feeling very exhausted. My oldest son told me that he would like to register me for a weekend church retreat held out of town. He had just attended a similar retreat and wanted me to experience it—and I said I would go.

That Friday, he told me to be at our local church's parking lot at 7:00 a.m. the next day to meet the bus but that he would not be home that night because he was attending a prayer vigil.

My son was in his second year of Catholic high school and was also completing his Catholic confirmation. As I had promised, I packed a bag, went to the parking lot near our home, and boarded the bus the next morning. It was a ninety-minute drive to the retreat center. Once there, I spent the next two days in Bible study with others at the retreat and had an enjoyable, fulfilling experience. Whenever we would leave for prayer and then return to our study area or meal area, we would find that our spaces were always cleaned and organized for us and that our food was always prepared. Sometimes, we'd be given letters of encouragement to read out loud—and some would be from my son. I was happy but wondered how this was all happening.

During the retreat, my tiredness went away, and I felt like I could fly. On Sunday, after a church service, it was time for us to have dinner. I was guided to a seat at a table and sat down. On the table was a paper placemat with writing and drawings, including a picture of an angel, and encouraging notes from lots of people, including my son. As I was reading my son's touching words, people started walking among us carrying candles. It was then that I saw my son with them, walking toward me. I was amazed and surprised and grateful all at once. Tears started covering my face. It turns out my son and others had secretly been there the whole time, arranging meals, cleaning our study spaces, and praying for us.

This was the message my son had written that had made me cry tears of joy:

Mom,

This is my gift to you, but you are the real gift—God's gift.

I just wanted you to know that I love you. I hope that the rest of your experience is wonderful and exciting. God Bless You.

Love,

Chris

I cried a bucketful of tears that day. Even thinking about it now makes me emotional and tearful.

With the help of my friends and my sons, and because of all my hard work, I graduated from the University of Minnesota in 1987 at the age of forty-one. I was able to keep moving toward my dreams.

During college, I had joined a number of governmental, women's, business, and professional organizations. In the years after my graduation, I was in a position where I could network with and eventually serve on many of their boards. Through one of my women's organizations, I even met board member and Minnesota Lieutenant Governor Marlene Johnson.

I nurtured these networks, and by the time I graduated I was appointed by the governor as the South Korean representative on the Council on Asian Pacific Minnesotans. I served in this role for five years.

I also began working closely with a former congressman who served as chairman of the Minnesota World Trade Center board. I was eventually able to get appointed to that board as well and served for six years. At the time, former South Korea Prime Minister Nam Duck-woo was the chairman of the Korea World Trade Cooperation, and I worked to build ties between Minnesota and Korea.

I also worked to build relationships with other organizations as well, serving on various advisory boards and committees. At the same time, I had begun setting up my own company, focusing on trading medical products between the United States and Korea. It felt as if I had to start over, like when I was first beginning college. I worked very hard, running around with the desire to succeed burning inside of me. Joining and working in many new organizations, I began to build a strong network, especially with other hard-working women. This became the work of my life. When I look back at my time as a student—working, studying, and raising my children for five years—I realize it was the most exhausting and active time of my life. My English was clumsy. Tests were difficult. Writing papers was even harder. Carrying my backpack filled with heavy books all over the sprawling university campus, I dreamed of a hopeful future for my family.

I am still grateful to my children's father. Even though we were divorced, we raised our children together. This gave me the opportunity to work and study. John always brought them to their soccer games and even coached some of their teams. John was a good father to our sons—there for the children as needed. He still is a good father and a good grandfather to our grandchildren. Today, John and I live close to each other, but we haven't seen one another for many years

For the five years I was in college, my daily routine was to get up at dawn, feed my two sons, send my oldest to school and my youngest to daycare, and then rush to the university campus. Throughout the day, I alternated between work and classes. At 5:00 p.m., I would pick up my youngest from daycare and come home. My oldest was usually already studying or watching TV at home.

After all these years of such a busy life, graduation day had come. At the graduation ceremony, I took photos with my children, aunt, and many friends. Afterward, we all celebrated—and I was thrilled that I had finally fulfilled my dream.

When I raised my sons, I usually made and fed them Korean food rather than western meals. Even when I cooked western food, kimchi and rice were always on the table. I believe this is why my sons still love Korean food so much.

Today, my oldest makes delicious Korean food. Everyone loves his food. He makes such delightful Korean meals, not just *bulgogi* (marinated beef), but also *ddakdoritang* (spicy chicken stew), *ddukbokki* (spicy rice cakes), *samgyetang* (ginger chicken soup), and various kimchis and stir-fry dishes. They are always very delicious. After he graduated from the University of Minnesota, he lived in South Korea and taught English for a year. This seems to have deepened his love and skill for Korean cooking. His delicious Korean food is loved by many people.

It is interesting to me because, when he was born many years ago, no Korean food was available in Minnesota. I could not even have the seaweed soup that, according to Korean tradition, a woman is supposed to eat after giving birth. This is not only a Korean tradition, but it also provides important nutrients and is excellent for the woman's health. When I gave birth to him, I could not have seaweed soup!

Now my son makes the most delicious seaweed soup for his friends when they are pregnant. He freezes it for them and tells them they should eat it after giving birth. Because he has many friends, he seems to make a lot of food for them.

I think food is essential in our lives. When we share food, we also share our love. When my sons were young, we were very poor, but we always had good meals together. I was very busy with school, work, and children. Even if I was yelling at my sons or we were busy, we always ate dinner together. I have always looked to rice meals for comfort. I have always believed in rice energy. To me, rice provides the body and mind the energy it needs to live.

As I write this, I am sitting and eating a Korean dinner with my dog Suni. I have been living in Minnesota for over fifty years. At home, I always eat Korean food with rice and kimchi.

My youngest works with me at our civil engineering company. He likes to come to my home to pick up Korean food that I make for him. His family lives close to me, and they love Korean food. I dearly love my son, his wife, and my grandchildren. It is very special to me that they eat my food and enjoy it.

My oldest son also works for our company. He has been working under contract with government transportation workers for almost ten years, and they all think he is an excellent Korean cook.

Sometimes, the companies they work for try to hire my sons. They could easily get jobs working for them, but they have chosen to continue working with their mother. I am grateful and proud of them. When the people they work with praise their work, this makes me happy. All our employees do high-quality work, and I am proud of all of them.

A few years ago, we invited about seventy guests to my seventieth birthday party and open house. My sons hosted the party and graciously greeted our guests. My oldest son made a variety of delicious Korean food throughout the day. It was wonderful of my two sons to give me such a nice birthday party.

***

In 1987, I was forty-one years old, and even though I had my degree from the University of Minnesota, I did not know if I would be able to find a job. Rather than fall into despair, I continued to take the necessary steps to continue with my life and find whatever job I could. This is a struggle that many people suffer through, especially immigrants.

Many immigrants in large cities turn to self-employment and find success there. Many highly educated Korean American immigrants were shut out of well-paying work in their chosen field due to systemic racism and anti-immigrant bias. People with master's degrees and doctorates in highly technical fields like engineering or medicine chose to become self-employed, opening small groceries, travel agencies, dry-cleaning businesses, and other similar businesses. Craftsman sometimes found it difficult to get into labor unions for more lucrative construction work, and instead had to take lower-paying jobs as day laborers.

I too had a difficult time finding work with a larger firm. I went to the Minnesota trade office and asked for advice. I discovered that one of the most active sectors in Minnesota was the medical-device industry. I decided to start my own company. I searched hard for work and found that 3M, a multinational company based in Minnesota, was buying IV injection sets overseas. At the time, they were using a Taiwanese subcontractor but were looking for a second source. By networking with some of the Korean international students at the university, I was able to get information about a Korean medical-device manufacturer called Green Cross. I contacted Green Cross and worked unpaid for a year trying to secure a contract between Green Cross and 3M. With a house and two children to feed, I had to work part-time as a waitress in the evenings while working on this contract and setting up my company.

I liked that this work was related to the medical field because it supports life. Securing a contract with a big company like 3M was a tremendous opportunity, but it was also very difficult and detailed work. Using my own funds, I made multiple visits to Green Cross facilities in Korea with 3M engineers from Minnesota. Quality and safety were of utmost importance, and I worked hard to make sure any requests or concerns from the 3M engineers were addressed by Green Cross. It was an arduous, year-long struggle—but after that year, they were finally ready to set up a contract.

The final hurdle was liability insurance. 3M usually required this of their manufacturers, but this type of insurance was either unavailable in Korea or prohibitively expensive. 3M asked to speak to Green Cross's legal representative to discuss this. Then I realized that Green Cross had put my name down as their legal counsel, which made me laugh out loud. I told them that was not my role. In the end, after a lot of effort, they settled on having 3M provide the insurance from a US company in exchange for a reduction in cost. The contract was signed, and we were in business. My company continued to oversee any issues with quality and shipping schedules, communicating with both parties on a regular basis.

I worked for ten years as a liaison between 3M and Green Cross. I also developed and maintained similar relationships between Green Cross and other large medical companies for twenty years, trading medical devices and facilitating technology transfers. I earned the trust of these companies. In fact, 3M eventually moved all their IV injection-set manufacturing over to Green Cross. Other large, multinational companies that I introduced also still work with Green Cross. For more than twenty years, this was the focus of my company.

In the 1970s, when I settled here, Minnesota felt like it was exclusively white. However, there have been major migrations to Minnesota, with about sixty thousand Hmong Americans who settled here as refugees from the Vietnam war and around fifty thousand Somali Americans. Today, about 20 percent of Minnesotans are people of color, but the people of color and immigrant communities here still suffer from acts of racism.

On New Year's Eve 1993, I was preparing food for a party. This was a positive time in my life. I had graduated college six years prior, and my medical-device trading business was in full swing. I rushed out to a local grocery store near my house to buy some items.

Because it was a holiday, the store was closing early and was packed with many people. As I stood in the long line of people with carts waiting to check out, a young white man in a suit and tie pushed me and shouted, "Move over!"

I replied, "Can't you see I have nowhere to move?"

He shouted back, "If you don't understand what 'move over' means, then just go back to China!" And then he stormed away.

I was most angry, and I followed him and shouted, "Look! Maybe you should go back to elementary school and study geography again. People who look like me are not all Chinese! You want me to go back where I came from? Okay! Let's all go back! Why don't you go back to your family's graves and dig up their bones and go back where? To

Germany? To Switzerland?" To my surprise, the other people in the store encouraged me, especially the women.

A year later, I became a member of the University of Minnesota's Board of Regents, and I was a keynote speaker at the Minneapolis College of Technology. My speechwriter suggested that I use this incident as the focus of a speech. I gave that speech with a trembling heart. Again, to my surprise, many people responded positively to this speech.

Despite these kinds of encounters, I do genuinely love Minnesota and its people—but I still live life like a porcupine. I still carry the tribal roots of the women of the Gyeongju Kims, and their brave thousands of years of history. I have lived here in America for most of my life, but I have not forgotten my past.

I can hear *CNN* playing on the TV in the background while I write this book. When I first came to the United States, the people on television seemed to talk so fast. I did not know many of the words, and I understood maybe 10 percent of what I heard. Now I can understand it all. I have worked many years to try to master the English language—and I still need to work at it every day.

Every morning, I listen to the news on the local public radio station. They provide local and world news, as well as economic, political, and social news. I listen to the radio while I am driving and try to repeat and mimic what I hear. If there are words I do not know, I look them up in my dictionary. I do the same with television, watching a lot of national and international news programs and current events. When I give a speech, I look up all the words I do not know and practice pronouncing them.

I also like to read a lot of magazines, newspapers, and books about various topics. I learn more and more every day about the language and about the world. I enjoy movies in English and television programs on *PBS*, *BBC*, *CNN*, and *MSNBC*. I find this beneficial, but also fun and enjoyable.

I also pray every day and live my life with deep faith. I always try to have gratitude for the little things. There is a power in all things.

Even now, I am sincerely hoping and praying for a greater understanding of things.

By the time I finish this book, I will have forgiven my father and loved him again these many years after his death in North Korea in 1956. I want to say goodbye to him. I want to say, "Father, I love you! Now rest!"

I lost my family in Korea, but I received freedom. I am eternally grateful, even when I am feeling lonely, to be living in a free country and breathing its precious air. It is because I live in a free society that I am allowed to write this book. I thank God for that.

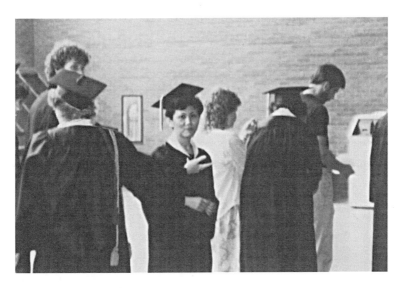

Spring, 1987 – Graduation from University of Minnesota,
University College
Credit: Photo Collection of Hyon Kim

Hyon Kim's mother's college picture *(first row, 2ⁿᵈ from left)*
Methodist Women's Christian College, Pyongyang
(what is now North Korea)
Credit: Photo Collection of Hyon Kim

Hyon's mother at Diamond Mountain, college years
(2nd from right)
Credit: Photo Collection of Hyon Kim

Hyon Kim with grandchildren, Ethan, Dylan, and Mia *(in front)*
Credit: Photo Collection of Hyon Kim

Hyon Kim's aunt with Hyon's sons, Paul (*left*)
and Chris (*right*), late 1980's
Credit: Photo Collection of Hyon Kim

Celebration of the 70th birthday of Hyon Kim's aunt, 1988
(from left to right, top row) Katie (Paul's spouse). Hyon
(bottom row), Chris, Aunt, Paul
Credit: Photo Collection of Hyon Kim

CHAPTER SIX

In the Spring of 1990, some surprising news came to families like mine scattered throughout the world. The North Korean government extended an invitation to people from separated families, giving them a chance to visit their families in the North for fifteen days.

It was during the spring of 1950 that I left home with my maternal grandmother at the age of four. The landscape was beautiful and green with flowers blooming everywhere. I grabbed my grandmother's hand, ran out the door, and hopped down the stairs.

In the forty years of being separated from my family, this was the first opportunity to see them in North Korea—and it came as a complete surprise.

It was 1989, and I had been frequently traveling to South Korea for business. When I did, I used the Han Travel Agency to purchase my plane tickets. Once, when I was having coffee with Mr. Han, the conversation became about my sad family story and how I was separated from them during the Korean War.

After my five years of college, I was busy running my medical-device trading company. Before that, right after graduation, I worked as a financial planner and stockbroker. However, it was tough to break into this market as a petite Asian woman. It was a very white, male-driven environment, making it difficult for me to get customers, so I ended up quitting. After that, I tried to get a job with a big company but was unsuccessful. So I decided to go into business for myself.

I traveled to Korea often for my medical business and frequently used Mr. Han's travel agency. Sadly, he passed away many years ago.

He was a very nice man with a thick North Korean accent. He had escaped down to South Korea during the war.

When I went to Mr. Han's office to buy a plane ticket, we would always sit and have a cup of coffee. Often, we only exchanged small talk and current events. He also spoke highly of my accomplishments and how impressed he was that I was able to graduate from the University of Minnesota as a single mother of two young children.

When I told him about my family in North Korea, he was surprised. "I did not know you had such a family story! Tell me every detail, including every family member's name. I'll contact North Korea and see what I can find out."

I was surprised to hear this. I made a phone call to my aunt to get things straightened out and gave all the information to Mr. Han.

Then, less than two months later, I got a call from Mr. Han. "You should sit down," he said.

I did not know what he was going to say, but I did as he asked.

"I just heard from my friend in Pyongyang. They found your family."

"Really?" I was in disbelief.

"Yes! Really! I have more information for you. Please come to my office as soon as you can."

In shock, I immediately rushed to his travel agency.

"How did you find out this quickly?" I asked as I sat down in his office.

"I know some important people in Pyongyang. It's easy for them to find people in North Korea because everyone's personal information is kept by the North Korean government."

I could not tell if I was happy or sad. I just felt numb as I sat there and absorbed this news.

"There's a big event in Pyongyang this spring. Do you want to go and see your family then?"

"What event? Can I really go to North Korea?" It seemed impossible.

"Yes! It's an event for families separated during the Korean War. Families like yours will gather from all over the world. Some of our most famous masters of traditional Korean music will go there too—Hwang Byungki, Kim Duk-soo, and Yun I-sang."

I could only think about the fact that I would see my family. My heart felt fluttery.

I knew that going to North Korea meant that I would be visiting an enemy of the United States. First, I checked in with the councils that I served on to make sure that I was allowed to do this, then I agonized over this decision all night.

The next day, I called the travel agency. "Mr. Han, I will go to Pyongyang."

I thanked him for his help in this matter, and I told him I would like to go to North Korea to see my family as soon as possible. In reality, the greatest motivation for this decision was that I wanted to go to North Korea and confront my father for abandoning me for the sake of his beliefs. I wanted to fight with my father and release all my hatred and resentment that I kept deep in my heart.

I wanted to scream at him: "What is more important to you, Father? Is it this rotten communist ideology? Shouldn't you take care of your family? I have lived a painful life because of you! I was a red, bbal-gang-i, communist child because of you! I cannot forgive you, father!"

I wanted to yell like that, and I wanted to pound on my father's chest.

I told my aunt about my trip to North Korea, and she said, "Yes, it's a good idea! Go! See your family. See your father." She shed tears of joy.

In the spring of 1990, after meetings with Green Cross Medical in Seoul, I immediately took a China Air flight to Beijing Airport to meet the group going to North Korea. All of us gathered there were living in various places in the United States; there was even a familiar face that I knew from Minnesota. Most of the people were elderly, except for a few that were closer to my age.

We first followed the group leader to a Korean-Chinese person's home in Beijing and ate Korean food. Then we went to the hotel and slept. The next morning, the group leader informed us of our schedule.

We were to meet at Beijing Airport and board a North Korean plane. The Soviet-made airplane was surprisingly old and rickety. The flight attendants handed out boiled eggs as a snack as the plane brought us to North Korea. Everyone on the plane just stared out the windows and said nothing. The air felt heavy in the silent cabin.

The flight arrived in Pyongyang sooner than I expected. The Sunan International Airport felt less like an airport in a capital city and more like a rural rail station in South Korea. When we got off the plane, several people were waiting for us. After passing through customs, I got a little scared as uniformed officers confiscated our US passports.

As we took a bus through Pyongyang, I heard a sad conversation from an elderly couple sitting behind me. The man said, "How has everything changed like this?"

"I don't recognize anything," his wife replied.

"Maybe it was all destroyed by bombing during the war," he added.

They looked out the window with doleful expressions.

The bus drove past the many tall statues that are all over Pyongyang, and then we arrived at the Koryo Hotel. Even looking at the beautiful chandeliers and general grandness of the Koryo Hotel, I could only think, *When can I see my family?*

The North Korean government was giving us the royal treatment. We ate a lot of delicious food at the Koryo Hotel. Beautiful women in fancy hanboks would always accompany us, but you could not talk to them or touch them.

We visited the famous Kumgang mountain area escorted by North Korean government officials. We watched the famous North Korean Mass Games with their thousands of performers. We visited Kim Il-sung University. And we ate delicious cold noodle soups at the famous Okryu-Gwan restaurant in Pyongyang.

One day, the North Korean government gave us headbands that they demanded we wear as we walked along the streets of Pyongyang. Suddenly, all these people were streaming toward us from every direction. They cried out for the reunification of Korea. They grabbed our hands and frantically shouted in our ears, "Let the poor South Korean people be freed and save them!" I still remember how uncomfortable it made me feel.

At the end, performing artists Isang Yun and Hwang Byungki took water from Baekdu Mountain in North Korea and Hanra Mountain in South Korea and symbolically poured it together. Just as Mr. Han had promised, we saw performances of traditional Korean music by Hwang Byungki, Kim Duk-soo, and others. Their performances were beautiful.

But over and over again, even during these incredible performances, my anxious mind wanted to know, *When do I get to see my family? When can I meet my father?*

Finally, the day came. On the twelfth day of my visit to North Korea, the government allowed us to see our families, but only for three days.

I had brought a lot of luggage from the United States filled with gifts to give to my family. With all this heavy luggage, I followed my North Korean guide toward Pyongyang Station. This guide was a member of the elite class who graduated from Kim Il-sung University. He was very kind to me. He told me my family lived in a big city and helped me get to my train. Like all the other North Korean officials, he called me Comrade Kim. We took our seats on the train and had many conversations.

At one point, he said to me, "It's a pity. Comrade Kim, if you had lived in North Korea, you would have graduated from Kim Il-sung University just like me. Let me arrange for you to meet our great leader, Comrade Kim Il-sung. Would you like to meet him?"

He asked me this repeatedly. I keep telling him that I was not nearly important enough nor qualified to meet him. I thanked him but firmly declined his offer. However, I kept thinking, *Why is he this eager to have me meet Kim Il-sung? Is it because I am on a state council in Minnesota? Is it because I am younger than many of the others?* Fortunately, they later switched him out with another guide. Perhaps this was because I would not meet with Kim Il-sung.

Finally, the train arrived at our destination. As I got off the train, I could see an older woman in a worn-out hanbok watching me. The man next to her looked like my older brother, but they did not make any gestures and were not allowed to come toward the train—we could only look at each other.

My aunt, who was very proud of my mother, always said to me, "Your mother was so tall. She wore wire-rimmed glasses and her women's college uniform. In her black skirts and white top, she was as beautiful as a bright, full moon. Whenever she played the organ and sang at church or whenever she was teaching her students, everyone would admire her beautiful and graceful appearance." This is also how she looked to me in the photos I had seen.

But the very skinny, little, white-haired old woman at the train station was nothing like how my aunt had described her. This was not the woman who was as beautiful as the moon. I watched her as I came off the train and felt nervous and tense. Finally, a few of the communist officials came and brought me to my mother.

With my older brother standing next to her, she looked closely at my eyes. Then she burst into tears. She whispered to me, weeping, "You have your father's eyes."

The communist officials brought us all to a different location. At this place, my whole family was waiting for me, including a younger brother I had never met. I wandered around looking for my father, the man I had come to see, the man I wanted to meet first.

But my mother quietly said to me, "Your father is not in this world. He is no longer alive in this world."

"Why? When?" I asked.

"It's been a long time. It was when your youngest brother was still in my belly."

I was stunned, disheartened, and disappointed. I did not know what to do. I just stood with my family and cried.

Thirteen people made up my family: my mother and my three brothers, each of which had three family members. They all seemed to live together in a small, single house. My mother later quietly told me that this was not their house. The government had moved my family into this house in anticipation of my arrival. This was apparently nicer than their actual house, but it was still very small, and its structure was poor. I slept on a small, hard bed in the smallest room. The other people in my family all slept together on the floor of the one other room.

The next day, I left my luggage with the children in the house and went out together with the Communist Party officials and my family. We had a welcome party, which I insisted on paying for, where we ate food and drank alcohol.

A communist minder was always by our side as designated by the North Korean government. This official wore a badge that said "Great Leader Kim Il-sung," and he followed me everywhere. After forty years of separation, we only had these three days together—yet it was nearly impossible for us to spend any time alone.

My mother would whisper things in my ears at midnight or take a chance to talk in the few moments we were alone. She spoke very cautiously about the truth of my father's death and her life as an underground Christian in North Korea.

My mother seemingly did not sleep during the three days I was with her. Every night, at a very late hour, she would repeatedly enter the room where I was sleeping, look at me, and lovingly put her hands on me. She was really sad—and the memory of this is very painful to me.

Every member of my family excitedly told me the story of the moment they heard that I was coming to visit North Korea. It reminded me of how Americans talked about the exact moment they heard about the Kennedy assassination.

At one point during the second evening, my family was sitting in a circle, playing a Korean tag game with a handkerchief. When I saw this, I was heartbroken because it reminded me that the people of North and South Korea were just the same people from the same country, even playing the same games. I remembered playing this game when I was young.

The game is like Duck, Duck, Goose in the United States. Everyone sits in a circle. In the Korean game, the person who is "it" has a handkerchief that they place behind one of the people sitting in the circle. That person must pick up the handkerchief and chase the person who left it there. If they do not catch them, they become "it." That evening, we also made the loser sing a song as a penalty. It was strange because the only songs my family members sang—even my adorable five-year-old nephew—were songs in praise of Kim Il-sung. They were the only songs they knew. It seems like North Koreans did not have any other songs to sing.

My mother was the only one to do something different. She recited a love poem called "Azalea," which my father had written for my mother. She quietly recited the poem as tears welled up in her eyes.

"The azalea blossoms are me. Your father wrote this poem for me because he said I was as pretty as azaleas . . ." She drifted off briefly, lost in her thoughts, then continued. "I was a widow at thirty-five. Since then, I've heard a lot of people talk about remarriage, but no one will ever know me like your father. How could I ever marry anyone else?"

As I listened to my mother, I pulled her into my arms and gave her a hug.

As we played the game, I would sing old Korean children's songs like "Icicle" and "Spring in My Hometown." My mother heard these and was moved to tears. She said that she had taught me those songs a long time ago.

That night, the two of us talked quietly. She continued to cry and whispered to me, "When I saw you standing, looking pretty, clasping your hands, and singing, I thought about how your father would be pleased and happy. He always called you his princess."

In front of my family, my mother never talked about my father at all. The North Korean government had executed him for treason. To mention his name would also be seen as treasonous.

The next morning, when I sat down in front of my small table to eat, I saw a bowl of rice with a few side dishes to eat. I looked at the larger family table and noticed nothing but thirteen small bowls of rice for the rest of the family. Then my mother came to me with an apple she held in her skirt. She handed it to me as if it were a small treasure. I put the side dishes and the apple on the family table. I broke down in tears and did not feel like eating. My family soon left for work and school for the day.

Then it was only my mother and my nephews in the house with me. My mother sent my nephews outside and locked the doors.

"You can't trust them!" she said. "Even the small children report you to the government."

She went to a chest in the dark corner of the room and took out an old notebook. "Why didn't you bring me a Bible?" she asked. "This old notebook is our Bible. Three of us who have been friends since we lived in Seoul wrote down all the passages we could remember. We really expected you to come with a Bible!"

I was shocked by this and could not say anything as I looked at those Bible verses scrawled into that small, worn-out notebook. By my mother's disappointed expression only lasted for a moment. She smiled and asked me to pray with her.

Tears poured down my face as I listened to my mother's prayers. My mother was thanking God and praying with gratitude. She spoke with delight that she had the chance to see me again before she died.

"How worried your father and I were when we left you alone in South Korea. We thought that you may have died or become a prostitute. When I see you like this, it is like a beautiful dream come true." With a sorrowful smile, she said, "I truly wish I could play hymns on the organ or piano again before I die. I wish I could loudly sing the church hymns, but that is just a dream. I will have to wait to do it in heaven.

"When you return to the United States, please be sure to go to church. I would like you to go to a Methodist church. I was a Methodist minister. Your dear grandmother, who is your father's mother, was a devout Christian and a Methodist deaconess until she died in Seoul. The homeless beggars could not even sneak past your grandmother's house without her feeding them."

I asked her about our family converting to Catholicism as my aunt had told me. She said that when my grandmother died, they were in a dangerous situation being communists. The Catholic sisters had helped our family survive, especially when my father was in prison. Because our family received a lot of help from them, they converted to Catholicism for a while—but she said our roots were always Methodist.

Then her face became very serious. "Your brothers become anxious and hate it when I talk about your father. They hate it even more when I talk about Jesus. They know we could all die if the wrong person heard us."

I was able to learn more about my father. The more I talked to my mother, the angrier I became. I could not believe my father put our family in this tragic situation. What a shameful person he was! Now I had even more hatred toward my father.

Later that day, my mother hurriedly took me out to a certain street, one that was far from any government escorts. She stood there and spoke to my father. "My dear husband, your daughter is here! She came here to see you. I know you were longing to see her and missed her until the day you died. You never forgave me, did you? I know you were angry because I sent her to visit my sister in Puyo."

She then looked around several times and quietly said to me, "This is where your father is. Your father, like everyone else on that day, was shot to death, executed. He was buried here in a mass grave."

I had no words. I thought about the many statues that I saw in Pyongyang. How could there be all those statues celebrating Kim Il-sung, but my father is just buried here under the street where people are constantly walking over his grave?

My father died in 1956 after being shot in the head. He was part of a group of South Korean communists that was purged by Kim Il-sung. As was Pak Hon-yong, he was accused of being a spy for the United States.

I stood there like a stray cat, a vagrant standing in the middle of this random street with my mother, wiping our tears, mourning my father's sins. Why could they not even allow my mother to find my father's body among the mountain of dead bodies so that he could be buried properly? What great sin did my father commit against Kim Il-sung and the Democratic People's Republic of Korea to deserve this treatment?

I thought, *My dear father, they buried you like an animal in a pile with other bodies in the middle of this street? Is this what your communist ideals got you?* I had this sudden urge to scream at him like an insane person. I wanted to swear at my father lying there under this unimportant street. I could feel my entire body break out in a cold sweat.

I wanted to turn around and leave North Korea immediately.

I was reunited with my family after forty years of separation, but I was only allowed to spend three days with them. Before I left my family in North Korea, I gave them everything I had with me except for the clothes and shoes I was wearing. Then I said goodbye, hoping that I would see them again someday.

On our last day in North Korea, we spent time in Pyongyang. As expected, the North Korean government held a lavish farewell party for us. At the reception that evening, they served us local specialties from different regions of Korea, as pointed out on a unified map of South and North Korea.

But this grand gala seemed very small to all of us. We had each met with our families and had come back sad and depressed. That night, a man from Chicago a little older than me got black-out drunk and did not speak. The next day, when I spoke to him in Beijing, he said he drank so much because he knew he had to resist shouting out "Kim Il-sung, you son of bitch!"

After fifteen days in the Democratic People's Republic of Korea, we arrived again at the airport in Sunan. Everyone was sitting and waiting get their US passports back. When it was my turn, the person handing out the passports said he could not give me mine. I was confused and shaken by this. "What do you mean?" I shouted.

"Comrade Kim has to live here in North Korea. Your guide, Comrade Choi, has fallen in love with you—you must marry him and settle down here."

I begged him to give my passport back. I told him I must go home and take care of my children and my elderly aunt. He then laughed and handed me my passport. He was joking. My body was shaking with fear from that awful joke.

Once we had our passports, we traveled to Beijing. The next day, we toured the Great Wall of China, but I could not take any pictures because I had left my cameras with my family in North Korea.

My father's recklessness drove himself and our family into a bottomless pit. Then my father, a young man of thirty-six, was ordered shot to death by Kim Il-sung. All of this happened because of my father's gross miscalculation about communism and Kim Il-sung.

In the 1940s, my mother—a college-educated woman, teacher, and Methodist lay minister—had a bright future. Because of her husband, she was stuck in North Korea, without her freedom. She struggled all her life and eventually died of starvation in 2002.

I remember my mother telling me a story in a resigned voice during my visit to North Korea: "When I was in Seoul, I once visited a fortune teller with your aunt," my mother said with a far-off look. "The fortune teller warned me, 'You will suffer while you live, and there will be no end to that suffering.'"

For the three days I spent with the family, every night was a sleepless night for my mother. Every night, she quietly entered my room and looked at my face. She did this countless times every night, as if she were engraving my face into her heart.

That is the last time I saw my mother. *She is always in my heart.*

Spring, 1990 – Trip to North Korea, Diamond Mountain
Credit: Photo Collection of Hyon Kim

Spring, 1990 – Trip to North Korea, Hyon Kim and her mother
Credit: Photo Collection of Hyon Kim

Hyon Kim's trip to North Korea, train station when first meeting her mother since she was 4 years old, 1990.
Credit: Photo Collection of Hyon Kim

CHAPTER SEVEN

When I returned from my visit to North Korea in 1990, I faced a major crisis in my life. Two years prior, I had married a white doctor who was eighteen years older than me. I think I was still looking at myself as Cinderella, searching for her prince. Turns out, I had made a bad decision.

After we were married, I began to see him for who he was—a miser and a racist. He was also a bit of a sexual deviant and expected me to comply to his urges. Once he wanted me to perform sexual acts on him while he was driving. I later learned he had affairs with hospital coworker nurses—the reason his first wife divorced him. I wonder if I was perversely drawn to him because of the sexual assault that I had experienced when I was young. In the end, I experienced a lot of the same emotions, hating myself and blaming myself for what happened. But after the incident in the car, I told him that I would tell everyone about him if he asked me to do something like that again.

He was known among his friends as a penny pincher and a cheapskate. This was also an issue in our marriage. He asked me to move out of my company's office and work from home to reduce costs. Every month, he would painstakingly review our personal bank statements and interrogate me like a criminal about every single cost. He would tell me I was wasting his money and that I should not abuse my position as his wife—it was his money.

I would only spend the money that I earned with my business. Even then, every time I bought cosmetics with my own money, I would rip off the packaging and sneak them into the house, ensuring they did not look new.

He told me specifically that he had millions of dollars in financial assets and that he was leaving me $300,000 in his will. Then, every time he flew out to his vacation home in Arizona, he would remark that I would get $300,000 for free if the plane crashed and he died. Every time he said that, I would ask him to remove my name from his will.

He would say racist things like "We should put all the Black people in boats and send them to Africa." He would take off his clothes while upstairs and throw them down to me on the main floor of the house, ordering me to take them to the laundry room, as if I was his geisha.

People think that being a doctor is a lofty profession. But when I saw him, I thought he was no different than a repairman who happened to know how to fix the human body. He had mastered the technical skills of being a doctor—but as for being a human being, he was very immature.

The worst thing he did was separate my family. Before we were married, both of my sons lived with me. Sadly, he allowed only my youngest son to live with us after we got married. In order to allow my older son to continue to live in the same house where we had all lived together, I gave the house to my ex-husband. I had been paying the mortgage for thirteen years; now I passed it on to my sons' father so my oldest could live with him.

But even then, the doctor was always cold and bossy toward my youngest son in a way that made me feel uncomfortable. Eventually, he also left to be with his father. Neither of my sons liked the doctor.

Before we were married, the doctor acted as if he enjoyed Korean foods, like kimchi. Later, he made me remove any kimchi from our refrigerator and store it outside because he was disgusted by the smell. At one point, during a fight, he pulled a jar of kimchi from the refrigerator and shattered it on the kitchen floor.

During the winter, he would keep the temperature of the house very low, requiring me to have to wear many layers of clothes. To keep the gas bill down, he would nag at me to not flush the toilets unless completely necessary. He treated me like this even though he was a doctor with money and prestige. He had a second house in Arizona where he often played tennis and golf.

I felt like I did not belong. I did not play golf or tennis. I was not allowed to do what I wanted in that house. It was not my home. However, I did not want to get a divorce, so I tried to live every day with positive thoughts about the future.

Then, in the spring of 1990, I went to North Korea to see my family—who I had not seen for forty years. I spent over ten thousand dollars on that trip, including travel expenses and the many gifts I brought to my family. It was all my own money, everything I had earned from my business.

On the day before the trip, realizing I had missed purchasing some gift items, I spent five hundred from our joint bank account. Then I took my fifteen-day trip.

When I returned to Minnesota, I was physically and emotionally exhausted. Many thoughts swirled in my head on the flight home, and I felt very sad about my life. When I returned, my husband was not interested in my trip. He was angry that I had spent $500 of his money without his permission before I left.

This confirmed for me that I did not belong in this place or in this marriage. I realized that I had made a mess of life by marrying him. I knew I had to leave. The next time he went to the Arizona to play golf, I packed up my stuff and left that house.

Once I divorced the doctor and moved back to an apartment near where my sons lived, both of my sons said that it took them two weeks to realize what it had taken me two years. He was a childish, selfish man. I laughed with sadness.

My dream of becoming Cinderella was once again shattered. The doctor was not my prince, just an ugly frog. My sons did not understand how much I didn't want to be divorced a second time. A woman who had been married to a GI and divorced twice would be the subject of gossip among the Korean American Christian community in Minnesota.

I never became Cinderella. I just repeated the same mistakes and suffered the same pain. Everything was just a continuation of the abuse I suffered as a child and have carried my entire life. Men were always like my father, who abandoned me for their ideals—or they were like my aunt's husband, who was both indifferent and abusive toward me.

I often wonder if I would be a different person if I had seen a therapist early in my life. I think discussing the abuse and trauma of my childhood may have saved me pain later in my life. I've never had a man in my life who loved me in a way that made me feel respected— I really thought I was undeserving of that type of man.

I discovered that I needed to find that respect within myself. I had, in truth, always been alone and supporting myself. Now I think of those experiences as precious assets that made me a stronger woman.

My divorce with the doctor was a straightforward one. I did not want anything from him—except to leave the house and the marriage as soon as possible. Ironically, my attorney charged me five hundred dollars. His lawyer accepted these terms and did not suspect me of trying to get anything from him. Years later, after he saw some stories about me become a university regent in the newspaper, the doctor's lawyer contacted me. He congratulated me on my success and said he had always known that I was a good person, even when he represented my ex-husband during the divorce. I was thankful for his kind words.

I remembered that he had also been kind to me during the divorce process. While my own lawyer seemed distant and slightly sardonic, the doctor's lawyer was warm and reassuring as I sat there in tears. From a very young age, I have been able to sense when someone is being disingenuous or judgmental of me—a result of the hardship and abuses I suffered as a child. I sensed judgment in my attorney on that day. I also sensed judgment among many in the Korean American community in Minnesota. Indeed, I became the subject of gossip among many in that community.

After my second divorce, another difficult decision came before me. I decided to break ties with my family in North Korea. After my visit, I had received letters from my family. In those letters were always pleas to send them money. Even my mother's letters asked for economic support from me. Not only is it illegal to send money to North Korea, but it is also pointless. It had been explained to me that if I were to send money, it would not make it to my family because North Korea monitors all correspondence. In truth, the government likely forced them to make those requests.

In the end, I made the sad decision not to write to my family. More than anything, I wanted nothing to do with the North Korean government, and I did not want my family to suffer based on anything I might say or do. For my protection and theirs, I cut ties completely.

***

In the winter of 1993, a colleague named Dr. DeLeon asked me to lunch. He was a Filipino American and the executive director of the Council on Asian and Pacific Minnesotans. I had been a council member and even served as chair up until 1992. During lunch, he made a big ask. He said that due to someone giving up her seat, a spot on the University of Minnesota Board of Regents had become available. The Minnesota legislature was going to quickly elect a new regent, and Dr. DeLeon, along with another local business leader, wanted to add my name to the candidate list. We needed to act fast because forty-two people had already applied, and they needed to get me to meet with the selection committee members.

I politely declined his offer. It seemed overwhelming to compete in a forty-three-person field, and I was already a member of the Asian Advisory Committee to the president of the University of Minnesota. Besides, it was a difficult time for me professionally as I was trying to raise funds for the small medical-device manufacturing facility that I owned.

But as I continued to listen to Dr. DeLeon's pitch, my heart was moved, and he persuaded me. The Board of Regents is a very important position, and it would give me the opportunity to help minority students at the university. At the time, out of twelve regents, only one was a minority. It is also a prestigious, sought-after position. Many famous and powerful people who love the University of Minnesota would be interested in sitting on the board. At the time, I happened to be living in the region that this seat would represent. I was told this was a unique opportunity, and I would probably never get another chance as good as this one. I eventually decided to take his advice and enter my name into the election.

The University of Minnesota was founded in 1851. Enrollment in 2020 was over fifty thousand students, making it the sixth-largest student body in the United States. It currently ranks fortieth in the Academic Ranking of World Universities. It is a large and influential research university, but it also plays an important cultural and civic role in the state of Minnesota. Among its alumni are two former United States Vice Presidents Hubert H. Humphrey and Walter Mondale. Faculty and alumni at the university have won a combined twenty-six Nobel Prizes.

I was elected as a member of the Board of Regents for the University of Minnesota in the spring of 1994. I was honored to serve as the first Asian American regent in the board's history. A monument on campus has every regent's name engraved into it, including mine. In the University of Minnesota's 168-year history, around two hundred people have served on the board.

Minnesota is a clean state filled with natural beauty. The Mississippi River begins in northern Minnesota at Lake Itasca. It has lush forests and more than ten thousand lakes and countless parks and nature preserves. Lake Superior, the deepest of the Great Lakes, sits in the northeastern corner of the state.

Starting in the 1600s, European settlers and French fur traders began to settle in Minnesota, pushing out the indigenous peoples like the Dakota and the Sioux. On May 11, 1858, Minnesota joined the United States as its thirty-second state. Its residents are primarily of Scandinavian and German descent. It is the largest state in the Upper Midwest, and it is culturally and economically important to the region.

When I arrived in Minnesota in 1970, the population was predominantly white, but there is historical and cultural importance to the Black communities that have lived there. For example, Roy Wilkins, an important participant in the Civil Rights Movement, grew up in the Rondo neighborhood in Saint Paul and graduated from the University of Minnesota, where he worked as a journalist and obtained a degree in sociology. Like Martin Luther King Jr., Wilkins was an active participant and significant figure during the March on Washington and the Selma-to-Montgomery marches. He served as the executive director of the NAACP from 1964 to 1977. Minnesota continues to have many important Black leaders, such as Dr. Josie Johnson, once described as the "First Lady of Minnesota Civil Rights."

A cultural stereotype exists about Minnesotans called "Minnesota nice." On its surface, it means that Minnesotans are polite and friendly, but the real meaning of the phrase—as experienced by many, especially people of color—is that Minnesotans are averse to confrontation and are cruelly passive-aggressive. The racism people experience in Minnesota is not necessarily open and nasty, but rather it is delivered with soft-spoken words and a kind face.

Minnesota has some of the largest inequities in the nation. A tremendous gap in educational and financial opportunities exists between whites and people of color, as well as between upper-middle class families and poorer families. Minorities, especially Black people, are disproportionately overrepresented among lower-class households and in the prison population. Currently, minorities are about 20 percent of Minnesota's population. This is higher than when I moved here in 1970, but the inequities for these groups continue to exist.

Minnesota is known for its large-scale farming and is a leading producer of corn, soybeans, and some livestock. Ninety-five percent of the farms in Minnesota are owned by white males. It is in these rural areas that you will sometimes find more conservative politics and white nationalism.

However, many progressives also live in the state of Minnesota—people who oppose racism and work to improve the lives of refugees, immigrants, and minorities. Many live in the urban centers like Saint Paul and Minneapolis. They are welcoming not just because they are compassionate, but because they recognize the contributions that immigrants and refugees bring to a community.

Among all the states, Minnesota has the highest number of refugees per capita. The refugee population has been estimated to be as high as 300,000 residents. Large Hmong and Somali communities live in Minnesota, primarily consisting of refugees and their families from both of those populations. Many people from these communities have become active in local, state, and federal government. They are also getting jobs in professional fields. Immigrants, minority groups, and refugees are an important part of the Minnesota economy and government.

In the winter of 1993, I was serving on an advisory committee to the president of the University of Minnesota. I felt it was important to provide my perspective as a minority and as an Asian American woman. My primary concerns were racial equality, women's rights, public access, and student empowerment. Seeing that there was good I could do as a regent, I eventually accepted Dr. DeLeon's invitation and submitted my application. When I saw the list of the other forty-two applicants, I noticed that most of them were white men. To be successful, I was not only going to need the support of Asians, but also of mainstream, more conservative whites.

I went to a former Minnesota state senator I knew for some advice. After a few drinks, he sneered at me with his slightly drunken face and told me I would never make it. He saw me as an Asian woman, an army girl, and an ex-bartender. He did not even think I should try. I was a little shocked by this, but he was a bit of a racist.

"What about you?" I replied. "You were just a little farm boy fresh from the cornfield. How did you become a senator?"

I went to see another friend named Ken. His wife was the executive director for Senator Paul Wellstone's Minnesota Office. I was a great admirer of Senator Wellstone. Ken and his wife were truly good people who strongly worked to support and uplift minority communities.

I told Ken about my conversation with the former state senator, including my response to his condescending remarks, then asked him if he thought I should run. He smiled, laughed loudly, and said he would help me. At the time, he was working as an attorney, but he had previously held a directorial position with the City of Saint Paul. He and his wife were plugged into the political community in Minnesota.

The 201-member Minnesota state legislature is charged with electing the twelve members of the University of Minnesota Board of Regents—eight from each of the congressional districts and four at-large positions. Regents are elected to a six-year term. The seat I was interested in had been resigned by a member who had decided to run for US Senate, and forty-three candidates were challenging for it. The winner of this election would have to serve out the remaining four years of that former member's term rather than the full six years.

The purpose of the Board of Regents is to establish policies and implement a present and future vision for the university. They also have the power to hire or remove the university president and approve budgets and financial plans for the individual colleges and programs. The annual budget for the University of Minnesota is currently about $3.5 billion. In 1994, it was a little under $3 billion. A board member was also required to be present at all graduation ceremonies to confer the degrees to the students.

Ken became my regent election adviser. In the weeks leading up to the election, I would meet him at the Minnesota State Office building at eight o'clock every morning to introduce me to as many of the 201 members of the state legislature as possible. We focused many of the one-on-one meetings on the Democrats. I would sit in their offices, listen to their concerns, discuss my views, and ask for their votes. I remember a number of these lawmakers excitedly bragging about their adopted children from Korea and showing me photos. I was also brought to a Republican meeting room and had similar discussions on a larger scale. With Ken's guidance and the help of Dr. DeLeon and other supportive Asian American friends and people of color, I made it through the first stage of the selection process. When the regent selection committee announced their short list of candidates, I was one of the eleven people on it.

After another series of hearings and caucuses, and with the support of a variety of lawmakers and other influential people, I became one of two final candidates. My opponent was a white man who was a well-known Minnesota Democrat. It still seems impossible that a petite Asian woman like me would have any chance against a man with his power and influence.

I think some expected me to step down at this point, but I had come too far. I was trembling with fear but was gaining confidence as I gained support. I am still grateful that I received the full support of Senator Sandy Pappas, who was a powerful female senator in Minnesota both then and now.

Another well-known senator boasted quite a bit of influence in the Democratic Party—and he supported the other candidate. We headed for a final confrontation at the State Capitol, and all the members of the Minnesota State House and Senate gathered to cast their vote.

So, what were the results?

I received 169 votes to my opponent's 32 votes. My sons and I sat in the observation gallery and listened to legislators say my name over and over again. At one point, my sons had counted fifty times in a row that someone said "Kim!" It was a thrill to hear my Korean name echoing through the capitol chamber.

Once the roll call was complete, the speaker announced the results of the election. I was sitting with my two sons on both sides in the upper-level observation gallery. The members of the legislature turned to me and gave me a standing ovation. I stood up and asked my sons to stand with me.

I was a war orphan and a bbal-gang-i at the age of four. I served in the South Korean women's military and struggled to finish high school at night in South Korea. I came to Minnesota and worked as a bartender, then as a keypunch operator, making a living for my family. I enrolled at the University of Minnesota at age thirty-five and then graduated at the age of forty-one. Now, seven years later, I had received this great honor. It felt like a miracle.

I prayed in my heart, *Thank you, God, thank you, my Lord! God Bless America!*

After the election, when I walked out into the capitol rotunda, ten to fifteen reporters flocked around me with a microphone. I felt excited and embarrassed at the same time. I thought about how important this seat was. I thought about how much the people of Minnesota loved the University of Minnesota. A few moments later, a woman appeared and introduced herself as the executive director of the regent's office.

The next morning, each newspaper carried news about the election. One of the headlines said, "Bartender to Ivory Tower." They used my job fourteen years ago to sensationalize my appointment. In the university newspaper, an editorial cartoon depicted the state legislature as a giant chicken succumbing to cries for diversity. In the United States, the chicken is used as a symbol of cowardice. The general tone of these articles was to depict me as incompetent—and my election as a symbolic gesture of racial diversity.

I thought about these articles. For the past few months, I had been working very hard to gather support for the election. Now I felt a little miserable as my accomplishment was being belittled. Then I remembered my life as a four-year-old child of a communist and how I was almost killed. I thought that this was nothing compared to that. I knew I would be okay.

Besides, even if I was a token appointment, even if the state of Minnesota sent me to the University of Minnesota just because I was a minority and a woman, I was still going to work hard. I knew what it was to be a struggling student at the University of Minnesota. I was going to work on behalf of those students. I felt like that was the real reason I had been given this opportunity.

The first day I visited the university as a member of the Board of Regents, I reconnected with the executive director of the regent office who I had met at the capitol, and I also met the other office staff. Then I attended my first Board of Regents meeting. The president of the University of Minnesota stood up and officially recognized my appointment by the state legislature. A few friendly faces attended my first meeting, including my two sons, a Korean pastor, another supportive friend, and Senator Sandy Pappas.

The Regents would meet twice a month. Presentations would be given by the university president, some of the college deans, and hundreds of other people with vested interests in university business.

Early on in my term, a new executive director, Steven, started working at the regents' office. I am always thankful for the moment Steven came into my life. The Lord has always brought me the right people at crucial points in my life, and Steven was such a man.

During my first meeting with Steven, he helped me navigate a pile of documents I needed to review. I told him what issues were important to me—issues like racial equality, women's rights, student empowerment, and public access. He pointed me to the documents that were most relevant to issues that mattered to me.

Steven really understood me and was always very good to me. We had many interesting and productive discussions. In the four years we worked together, we developed a good relationship. I felt like he was family. He even reminded me of one of my brothers in North Korea. A few years ago, he and I visited Korea together.

Steven is also a hard worker and has held many important positions. Before coming to the University of Minnesota, he worked as chief of staff for US Congressman Tim Penny for more than a decade. He has since worked as senior staff for members of the US Congress, chief of staff to the Minnesota governor, and city coordinator for the mayor of Minneapolis.

For two days every month, I would attend all-day meetings with the eleven other board members. Once a month, the president of the university would have the regents and various corporate, nonprofit, and political leaders as his guests at the university president's residence for a semiformal dinner. I often brought my oldest son as my guest to these events. At the first dinner I attended, I was struck by how friendly and happy everyone was. Many people congratulated me. As I thought about those newspaper articles, I wondered who else viewed me as a token appointment. Knowing what I know about the passive aggression of "Minnesota nice," I often wondered what was behind those smiles.

Despite this suspicion, I have always been impressed by the level of respect given to members of the Board of Regents. From the president on down, people treated us with great respect. Even as a former regent, I am addressed by my title as a point of honor. Once my mail carrier asked me if I was a judge. He noticed that I would receive mail that had "the Honorable" before my name.

It honestly made me a little uncomfortable at first. But as I think about the 168-year history of the University of Minnesota and all the traditions tied into that history, including the long history of the Board of Regents, I feel honored to be a part of it. Once a year, the current president invites former board members to a dinner event at his official residence, with the current board and deans. I am honored and appreciative of this level of deference given to us and our contributions.

In the spring of 1996, the University of Minnesota wanted to award an honorary doctorate to South Korean President Kim Young-sam. I was asked to join a pre-award trip to South Korea and China. I joined a group that included the university president, his chief of staff, the vice president, the president of the Alumni Association, the head of the University Foundation, a Korean professor from Minnesota, and everyone's spouses. I was there as a representative of the regents.

The Korean professor worked with the chief of staff to plan the trip. In the process, he worked hard to belittle me and diminish my influence during the trip. In Seoul, he monopolized the president and chief of staff, riding in the same vehicle with them, while the rest of us followed along in a van. At events, as in our visit to the Korean president's chief of staff at the Blue House (Korea's equivalent to the White

House), I was intentionally seated away from any of the principal figures. During the official breakfast with the chief of staff, every other university official was presented with a gift except for me. A very clear distinction was being made indicating that I was not an equal part of the official delegation.

The university vice president was very critical of this treatment and spoke up on my behalf to the president. He said that it was the Board of Regents that approved this trip and allocated the money for it. He said that I was as much a university delegate as anyone else on the trip and that I was being treated very rudely.

During that time, I had been strongly pushing for increasing the scholarships for minority students. This stance had put me in conflict with the university president. Still, my experience during the trip was very disappointing, especially the condescending treatment I received from the Korean professor.

In another instance, the professor tried to cancel my speech to the University of Minnesota Korea Alumni Association. However, after the vice president and I protested, the speech was reinstated, and I gave the speech as scheduled. It was a frustrating experience, with another professor's wife wondering aloud how a person like me could have ever ascended to such a high position at the university. I was reduced to tears in front of the vice president, who tried to comfort me.

When I returned from that trip, I received an interview request from a reporter. They wanted to take note of this historic event: the first Asian American regent to visit Asia as a representative of the University of Minnesota. They wanted my reaction to being a part of history. I declined the request, saying I was too busy. The next month, when we traveled back to Korea to officially present the honorary doctorate to President Kim Young-sam, I requested that the chair of the Board of Regents accompany us.

The University of Minnesota has more than three thousand tenured professors, and they wield a lot of power. There is the University of Minnesota Foundation, which is greatly funded by Minnesota business leaders and other powerful members of the community. There is also the University of Minnesota Alumni Association. The Alumni Association and the University Foundation raise a lot of money for the university every year. All these groups work to influence and control the Board of Regents in their "Minnesota nice" way.

A leader in the Alumni Association was dismissive of me and sometimes laughed in my face. I had become very argumentative regarding scholarships for minority students. She treated me like a thorn in the university president's eye. She told me that the Board of Regents exists only because of the way the land-grant university was historically set up. She believed that it was our role to simply execute the vision of the president and rubber-stamp his decisions. She viewed me as inexperienced and naive about how the educational system worked. To her, I was still the bartender who climbed to the ivory tower.

I was again viewed as a token, a small symbolic gesture toward minority inclusion. Many thought that I would understand that this was my role—and thus willingly go along with their opinions, rubber-stamping their decisions. They were often friendly and polite, but it was superficial. Even Korean professors at the university ignored my position and treated me as if I knew nothing. Even here, I could not escape the condescension that many Koreans have toward women that married US soldiers. It was a surprise in the Korean community when I was elected to the Board of Regents. The Korean Society of Minnesota had many alumni from famous universities in Korea, but I had only attended high school in Korea. I came here with no college degree. I served as a woman in the Korean military. I had worked as a bartender in Minnesota. I was not a college student in Korea, so I could not belong to one of the many Korean university alumni associations in Minnesota. There was a snobbery among many educated Korean immigrants, as well as a kind of sexism at play. As a Korean woman, I was looked at as behaving too proudly and too strongly. I, in fact, was not even invited to participate in events for Korean alumni of the University of Minnesota.

This, of course, was not true of all Koreans—one Korean-born gentleman whom I admired was a partner at one of the largest law firms in Minnesota. He graduated from law school in Korea, worked diligently, and overcame difficulties to succeed in the United States. He was always kind and humble, a good role model for his children.

The environment in the Korean American society here is gossipy and judgmental. Many instances exist in which hard-working people are undermined by rumors, gossip, and even anonymous, defamatory letters to people in power. Even Korean pastors at Korean churches get cast out from their communities based on these dubious tactics.

I often wonder why some in the Korean community here find it so difficult to support one another. I think of the example of the Hmong American refugee community in Saint Paul. These people, who have lived for thousands of years in the mountains of Laos and Southeast Asia, came together in this cold land and worked together to build a community. Many Hmong people have become political and educational leaders in Minnesota and work to help their people.

During my time at the Board of Regents, some political leaders suggested that I run for office. In response, some Koreans wrote harmful and anonymous letters to try to get me to quit. To them, I was still just the loudmouth woman who married a US soldier.

Being a member of the Board of Regents is a prestigious position and a lot of hard work—with no salary given for this position. As a single woman running a small business, I had difficulty balancing all my work responsibilities with the important work I was doing at the university. It was a daunting task, but I performed it without ever giving up.

I had a lot of meaningful exchanges with University of Minnesota students during my time as a regent—students who believed in my leadership and my genuine concern for their well-being. One such student was Matt Musel, president of the Student Association. He considered me a mentor, and we are still in touch today.

In a recent discussion, he reminded me that I played a role in saving the scholarships of 1,500 minority students during my time at the university. He said the students were grateful for how I was able to work together with them. He said that I had listened to their voices in a way that others had not.

For me, hearing their voices was easy because their voices were my voice too. I was a single mother with two children and no money to attend school. During my time at the university, I was able to attend and graduate from school because of the types of scholarships that the university president was trying to eliminate. So now that I had a voice as a regent, I was going to be the voice for those 1,500 students.

Matt later told me that those minority students I worked with at the time, many of them women, have become strong leaders and activists, leading successful, extraordinary lives. This was such joyful news it brought me to tears. I am so proud of them and happy for them.

Here is Matt, in his own words, explaining the situation from his perspective.

On the Battle over Scholarships for Minority Students

A year after Hyon Kim was elected to the University of Minnesota Board of Regents, she would have her first major conflict with President Hasselmo over access to higher education.

In 1979, the university attempted to help students from diverse backgrounds by establishing the Office of Minority and Special Student Affairs (OMSSA) grant. The grants of $1,250 to $2,250 per student were given to historically educationally disadvantaged, economically disadvantaged, and minority students. In May of 1995, after the students had left campus for summer vacation, Hasselmo ended the $1.6

million funding of this grant, arguing that it was out of compliance with federal laws prohibiting the funding of race-based scholarships. The 1,500 students had their scholarship for the next year eliminated. The decision was made without student input, and students had been denied access to the information that led to this cut.

Student groups were the first to react, and on May 31, students on campus for the summer semester stormed the president's office in protest. Continuing through the summer, students formed a coalition to address the issues that were coming into effect because of these changes. Their slogan was "Right to an accessible education for students." Students were soon joined by civil rights and women's rights groups in opposing this cut to student scholarship.

As they prepared to challenge the university president's decision, students soon learned that they had a friend and champion in Regent Hyon Kim.

One of the most vocal student leaders was Darcy Louis, an American Indian student from Watertown, South Dakota. Louis was a junior in the College of Liberal Arts, majoring in American Indian Studies and leading the American Indian Student Cultural

Center. Louis was protesting at the president's office and learned that the Board of Regents was having an open forum on June 14th. Louis organized other students of color to attend the forum and speak to the regents. According to the *Minneapolis Star Tribune* article by Nancy Livingston, Darcy Louis told the regents' forum, "By maintaining a 'color-blind' student financial aid policy, [the University] is choosing to interpret federal financial aid guidelines in a way that will hurt minority students. The university has chosen to gut OMSSA and redistribute federal money in a different way. The money did go disproportionately to minority students, but not exclusively. If this university is going to be committed to diversity, it has to be committed through financial aid."

Louis was one of a half dozen students who spoke to the regents on that day. Regent Hyon Kim began to ask questions and advocate for these students. The social justice organizers now had a champion in the university leadership.

Within two days, Hasselmo offered to restore $400,000 of the $1.6 million that was cut from the OMSSA grant. This small victory was a response to Regent Kim's leadership. Hasselmo hoped that this small amount would satiate the concerns of students and Regent Kim, but the students continued to organize.

The next concession from Hasselmo was to create an advisory committee to investigate the issue and report back a solution. In universities, committees can be used to kill organizing through delaying a decision and allowing the passion to subside. Students demanded that the committee be comprised of 50 percent students and have a student co-chair. Students again found a friend in Regent Kim—and the students won their demand. Darcy Louis was selected by students to be the co-chair. Louis wrote, "Regardless of what is happening at a Federal level, this university made a promise for diversity. The promise was made not only in 1978 with the creation of these grants, but in 1995, that university is using the budget situation as scapegoat for their commitment to diversity."

— Matt Musel

I worked hard to support these minority students and get their scholarships back. Many of these students were the first members of their family to enroll in college. They came from poor backgrounds and could not afford school without these scholarships. I remember attending school when I was poor and raising two children. I could feel their desperation.

At the completion of the school year, the president had cut scholarship funding for the following year. Students who had been planning to come back in the fall would not have the money to continue their education. The move had been made when very few students were on campus to protest—but protest they did. By the end of the summer, two weeks before the new school year begin, there was still no resolution.

The day before the final vote on funding, I visited a school's vice president and said that we needed to come up with a solution that adjusted the budget and guaranteed that the students would not lose their money. He said that he could talk about it with me in the morning. I told him that was fine, but I was going to wait in his office overnight to make sure he talked to me first thing in the morning. After repeatedly pleading with me to go home, he made a promise to contact me with a solution. The next morning, he contacted me right away with a plan to save the scholarships. He and I gained a lot of respect for each other over this incident, and we have remained good friends. Again, from Matt's perspective,

> In July and August, the advisory committee met, and the students feared that their voices would not be heard. The students needed the regents again, and on September 7th, the Board of Regents asked to hear a report from the committee. The continued interest of the regents was necessary to keep the president's attention on the committee. On October 10th, the advisory committee made its final recommendation—restore the entire $1.6 million in OMSSA grants to students. While the students were proud of their work, the president had not agreed to restore the

funding, and the final decision was left to the Board of Regents.

On October 12th, the Board of Regents met, and with Regent Hyon Kim as the champion for students, the board voted to restore the entire $1.6 million to students. In the school newspaper, the *Minnesota Daily*, Darcy Louis, a Native American student who went from protester to committee chair stated, "This is awesome. I'm just sharing right now; I can hardly talk."

With the leadership of Hyon Kim, the president's proposal to eliminate student scholarships was defeated.

– Matt Musel

Another incident involved the General College at the University of Minnesota. The General College was an important way for disadvantaged students to access the university. Minority students, immigrants, students with difficult backgrounds or less access to education were given a chance at a university education by attending the General College. I myself was a product of the General College. The president wanted to eliminate the General College in order to bring more focus to the university's role as an elite research facility and university. Just like with the scholarships, the very thing that the president and the people in power wanted to eliminate was not only something I believed in, but something that had directly helped me when I was a student.

On the Battle over Access to the University and the Future of the General College

The university has trained the establishment leaders of government and business, and it has been the center of organization for civil rights, racial equality, and women's empowerment. Historically, the university chose to be an accessible institution of immigrants, low-income people, and the disadvantaged.

Enter the Korean immigrant. With her election to the Board on April 21, 1994, Hyon Kim became a champion of access on the inside of the Board of Regents. Her leadership would change this quiet and conservative board into an active board. With her example, the board became confident in challenging the direction of the university president.

For the champions of access at the university, their biggest victory happened four months after the OMSSA vote: Hasselmo announced his retirement as university president. He was providing a year's notice to allow time for a search for a new president.

Many thought that Hasselmo's retirement announcement signified the end of his quest for a more elite student body.

This was not so! Hasselmo was still committed to make a more exclusive university. A month after this retirement announcement, on March 26, Hasselmo decided to close the largest door for access to people of color to the university —General College.

General College is an access point to the university for students who may not meet the competitive admission standards of the other colleges.

The college offers a variety of support services that address the needs of students with diverse backgrounds and characteristics, including urban students, first-generation college students, student parents, students with disabilities, students of color, older students, and non-native speakers of English. Enrollment is approximately 1,800 students, with 850 new students joining the returning students each fall.

On Tuesday, April 9 there was a massive student rally in support of General College.

On Thursday, April 11 Students were unsure of how the Board of Regents would vote on this proposal, but students trusted Regent Hyon Kim. At times, Regent Kim was the only regent that they trusted.

On Friday, April 12, the Board of Regents voted nine to one to support General College and to defeat

Hasselmo's proposal. The students and their supporters held a large rally in support of General College. Regent Hyon Kim attended with her fellow regents. The loudest applause was for Regent Hyon Kim, but she shared the credit generously with the other regents. Board of Regents Chair Thomas Reagan stated, "The current process of evaluating the General College has been flawed and is not productive. It should be stopped."

– Matt Musel

No sound financial reason existed to eliminate the General College. The professors would have to be reassigned to other programs in the university, so there were no savings there. And with an annual budget of nearly $3 billion, the $4 million allocated to the General College was hardly a financial burden. This massive elimination of opportunity to minority and disadvantaged students was a huge moral price to pay for something that barely made a difference in the overall budget—but this was the constant war I was fighting.

The time that I was on the Board of Regents was a challenging time. There is a vast network of wealth and power among many alumni and other people associated with the University of Minnesota. As a struggling, self-made woman, and as the only Asian woman on the Board of Regents, I stood outside that culture of power and wealth. However, because of my position at the board, they were reluctantly forced to interact with me. It was made clear early in my term that I was expected to follow the lead of those in power. Unfortunately, I could not do that. I considered my position and my perspective important to the university. I worked hard at my job, thinking about why I had run for the position on the Board of Regents in the first place. Because of this, I was looked on as an antagonist of the president that they supported. The people in power blatantly looked down on me and ignored my input. I dealt with their arrogance and condescension during my entire term.

In the end, while I was being pressured and ostracized by those who wanted me to fall in line, I continued to work hard on behalf of the students and the marginalized communities of which I saw myself as a part. My supporters encouraged me, saying that the marginalized voices need to be heard in a state-supported university system. But it was difficult to fight against the power and wealth of the status quo.

To add to this, an even bigger issue in my life at the time was the state of my company. The income from my company was how I made a living, but I became too focused on my university work that I neglected my own business. The small-scale manufacturing facility was struggling to find steady work, and I was running out of capital, meaning that we were trying hard not to close the company's doors. When the time came to run for reelection on the Board or Regents, I could not consider it because I needed to focus on my company.

When I announced that I would not run for reelection, some of the university president's backers took the opportunity to smear my name and belittle the decisions made by the Board of Regents during my time there. Editorials appeared in the local newspapers parading as "objective" viewpoints, demeaning the very issues that were important to me. I was hurt and angry but could no longer fight against it without my position on the board. This is the type of "Minnesota nice" racism many people here experience. It was one of the worst moments of my life.

As this was happening, my company was in an even more dire situation. One of my primary investors called a board meeting and ordered me to step down as president and remove myself from day-to-day operations. They were going to hire the man who was the vice president at the time to operate the company but keep me on as owner to maintain our minority, woman-owned status as a disadvantaged business enterprise. Not only was this unethical, but it was illegal. I refused, lost investors and much of my management staff, and tried to keep the business afloat by myself. Sadly, I eventually had to shut it down. I was exhausted and penniless.

In the aftermath of all this, I lived every day in a life of loneliness and despair. I often felt suicidal. I hated Minnesota with its long, cold winter and its passive-aggressive people. It felt like everyone I talked to had two faces: a polite one that they showed and an ugly racist one that they hid from you. I know that it was not everyone, but I felt as if I was dealing with people like that everywhere I turned.

I became listless. I spent my time singing in Karaoke rooms. I invested in and ran a small sushi restaurant that closed after a couple of years. I was self-destructive and unfocused. I went out of my mind with my loneliness.

I missed my mother and my family in North Korea very much. I do not really remember how many years I lived like that. Eventually, I began to wake up and work to get myself out of this destructive routine.

And as I gradually recovered my life, my two sons stood beside me. I began to rediscover how much I really loved my sons and their families. Now the three of us have been working together building my civil engineering company for the last ten years. We also have employed several immigrants—civil engineers with high levels of experience and training who have difficulty finding employment in the United States. They work hard for my company. I feel a special kinship with them because they were looking for opportunities just as I had in the past. Some wonderful Minnesotans work with me too. It is a joy to interact with my staff every day. I also get to meet many people when I am networking and marketing our company. We are a small company, but we do work for government agencies and large corporations. Our company is slowly growing and thriving.

America is a country that strives to give everyone an opportunity. My company benefits from organizations and laws that try to uplift disadvantaged businesses like mine, run by a minority woman. It is a system that tries to extend the American dream, so it applies to all people. More could be done, and I am often critical of this system. Even so, there is more fairness than there has been in the past—and more opportunity. I truly believe that if I work hard, I will have a chance to achieve success. I am grateful to be living in a country where that is true.

Spring, 1995 – First Lady Hillary Rodham Clinton
University of MN – College of Liberal Arts Commencement
Left to right: Sheila Wellstone, First Lady Hillary Rodham Clinton,
U.S. Senator Paul Wellstone, UMN Regent Hyon Kim
Credit: Photography provided by the University of Minnesota, used
with permission April 1, 2022

Hyon Kim with sons Paul (*left*), Chris, and her Aunt
in St. Anthony, MN, 1994
Credit: Photography provided by the University of Minnesota, used
with permission April 1, 2022

Radio Program on the impact of Asians in Minnesota, St. Paul
(left to right) Regent Hyon Kim,
Governor Jesse Ventura, Dr. Bruce Corrie, 1996
Credit: Photo Collection of Hyon Kim

Visit to Japan on route to South Korea, 1996
(*left to right*) Vice President Walter Mondale, Ambassador to Japan;
President Nils Hasselmo, UMN; Ms Joan Mondale;
Hyon Kim, UMN Regent; UMN Alumnil Ms. Patricia Hasselmo
Credit: Photo Collection of Hyon Kim

University of Minnesota Board of Regents, 1995-1997
Hyon Kim *(second from right)*
Credit: Photography provided by the University of Minnesota, used
with permission April 1, 2022

Spring, 1995 – First Lady Hillary Rodham Clinton
University of MN – College of Liberal Arts Commencement
Credit: Photography provided by the University of Minnesota, used
with permission April 1, 2022

EPILOGUE: HEALING AND RECOVERY

I have lived in Minnesota for fifty years. While living in the United States, I have watched countless Korean dramas and other television programs. Korean dramas were often a welcome distraction from all the difficulties I experienced in my life. They served as an oasis from my struggles with the English language or American customs. Korean dramas have been a big part of my life, bringing me laughter and tears.

I especially love how these shows portray the importance of family even in the face of hardships. If you live a difficult life, you do so together, under one roof as a loving family. I especially loved one drama called *Trap of Youth*. It was written by the famous writer Ms. Kim Soo-hyun. I watched it weekly and cried many tears. The female protagonist loses her parents in an accident when she is very young. Then her aunt, uncle, cousin, and grandmother take her into their home and raise her. I especially loved the grandmother, who was warm and caring. I thought of my grandmother who had died during the Korean War. I believe that if she had lived, my grandmother would have wrapped me in the warmth of her love and protected me just like the one in the television show.

More and more, I have become grateful for the small things in life. I live with my small dog Suni, and I love her very much. I love my company. It is a joy to interact with my staff every day. I also get to meet many people when I am out networking and marketing.

And when I think of my two sons, I feel like I have the whole world. I am most proud of my sons. I have always dreamed of working with my two sons to grow the company. I am grateful to the Lord and will serve Him diligently until He calls me.

It is now late January of 2021. I am seventy-four years old. Soon it will be Seollal, the lunar new year. It seems like the years pass by too fast, like flowing water. I am preparing the menu with plans to cook traditional Korean food for the holiday.

I must make rice cake dumpling soup, beef *bulgogi*, and other special dishes for my sons, my daughter-in-law, and my grandchildren. They all love Korean food and happily eat it. This time, I am going to make the rice cake dumpling soup with a generous amount of beef ribs. Korean food requires a lot of work in the kitchen. Still, it is one of the ways that this Korean mother and grandmother can truly express the love she feels in her heart.

I always need a lot of patience and must spend many hours when I cook Korean food. As I slowly clean and prepare the garlic, I think about the patience of Korean women. I think about the lives of all the Korean mothers and grandmothers. I wonder how much time they have spent in their kitchens feeding their families.

I love how much my youngest son and his family enjoy my food. I sometimes send beef *bulgogi* and kimchi *jjigae* (a stew with pork, tofu, and kimchi) home with my youngest son, along with a jar of homemade kimchi. I am proud of my oldest son, who enjoys making Korean food and does it very well. My oldest likes to take me to the theater and fancy restaurants for my birthday or as a Christmas gift. I love inviting my friends and people from my church to my home where I serve them Korean food. Last year, a promising young North Korean refugee studying at a university in the United States visited me over her winter break. I cooked Korean food for her and her friends. I enjoyed my time with them as well.

In 2014, I became intensely interested in the lives of North Korean refugees. These are our people, our brothers and sisters who have escaped from the repressive regime of North Korea. It is one of the most overlooked and most vicious human rights tragedies in the world, a social justice blind spot on a global scale.

I met one woman who lived secretly in China for fifteen years. As a North Korean refugee in China, she was living there illegally and had no rights. North Koreans in China are immediately sent back to North Korea by the government—so they must live in hiding. Fortunately, she has escaped China and now lives in South Korea. For her and countless others like her, some of whom I have met, I created a non-profit organization called the Midwest Alliance for North Korean Refugees (MidANKR) that helps North Korean refugees. www.RefugeesNorthKorea.org.

In 2015, we held our first big event, a symposium to raise awareness and educate people about this human rights crisis. It was held at the University of Minnesota Humphrey School of Public Affairs and was well attended. Several speakers were featured, including people from *Now on My Way to Meet You*, a South Korean television show in which North Korean refugees come to share their experiences with a panel of Korean celebrities and other prominent figures. In the show, they discuss the horrors of life in North Korea and tell their stories of escape. We invited the producer of the show, the head writer, and a young North Korean refugee named Praise Ju, along with other South Korean human rights activists. We also invited a US human rights activist, a US congressman, and a Minnesota senator.

We held a second symposium the following year with other refugees and human rights figures. We are also working to support North Korean refugees who want to study English in the United States. We have worked with various human rights activists in Minnesota, including groups led by the pastor at my church. Many people in Minnesota want to serve their neighbors and help those who have lived hard lives worldwide. In our church, we have helped refugees from around the world, treating them like members of our own families.

I am incredibly grateful to the organizations and churches in my community that have expressed interest in helping North Korean refugees. Although we are a small organization, we work with a passionate group of volunteers to discuss how we can help North Korean refugees and educate Americans about their human rights issues.

In July, I will turn seventy-five years old. There are still many things left to do—and to say. This makes me happy because I know I will continue to accomplish things and continue to write.

I have come to the end of this story. I do not see it as a story of a successful woman. It is a story of survival. It is the story how a young orphan, a bbal-gang-i, red, communist daughter abandoned at the age of four in the middle of the war, found a way to survive.

Now that it is all written down, I feel lifted. The heaviest burden I have carried throughout my life was the hatred and resentment I held deep in my heart for my father. After learning about him from my mother in North Korea, I have forgiven him in the course of writing this book. Hating my father was a heavy burden, a giant stone in my heart. Now I am pushing up feelings of love and compassion from the depths of my heart to him.

I truly feel encouraged by the life I have lived so far—and the life I have yet to live. I feel like I have a chance at true, lasting happiness. Perhaps the last years of my life will be the most blessed years. Thank you, my Lord, my God.